THE CUTTING EDGE

Critical Questions
for
Contemporary Christians

THE CUTTING EDGE

Critical Questions
for
Contemporary Christians

VOLUME 2

Compiled by

H. C. BROWN, JR.

WORD BOOKS, PUBLISHER
Waco, Texas — London, England

TO

My colleagues and friends

who have taught and who now teach

Christian Ethics

at

Southwestern Baptist Theological Seminary

T. B. MASTON

RALPH PHELPS

C. W. SCUDDER

WILLIAM PINSON

CONTENTS

ACKNOWLEDGMENTS

A special word of appreciation must be given to these friends who have made these two books possible:

The twenty contributors

Mr. George Baskin

Mrs. Velma L. Brown

Mrs. Iris Harris

Mrs. Linda Lowe Leech

Mrs. Phyllis Spears

Dr. C. W. Scudder

Dr. William Pinson

INTRODUCTION

The Cutting Edge: Critical Questions for Contemporary Christians, in volume one shows twelve facets of the race question, while in this second volume fourteen other critical ethical issues are discussed. This data is presented in the form of *essays, speeches, lectures, talks,* and *sermons.*

The twelve facets of race in volume one and the fourteen issues presented here do not represent all the ethical questions of our day. These fifteen critical questions do, however, represent some of the more disturbing problems, issues, and ideas agitating the minds and hearts of modern-day Christians.

These fifteen issues represent the areas where contemporary Christian churches need to "get involved." They show the places where Christians can become part of the "cutting edge" of true Christian faith in action. On a recent television show a cowboy said to a priest as they spoke about God and faith, "Padre, I just don't understand how you can put all of those [God and faith] under a steeple!" One major problem with contemporary Christianity is that it does indeed seem to try to put God and faith under the roof of a church—"under a steeple!"

How utterly tragic such an absurd attempt is: God and faith restricted and confined under anyone's church steeple! God and faith cannot be confined to a building, a church, a denomination, a nation, or even a race. Nothing but sterile religion can result from any attempt to control or to institutionalize God and faith.

On the contrary side, a live, vital, and relevant practice of Christianity demands that Christians, churches, and denominations be in the world. They need to entangle and to involve themselves with people as they are dealing with disturbing problems and issues. Nothing less is the practice of pure Christianity.

May God lead all of us to seek his will as we give answer for ourselves to the critical issues of our day.

Above all, may each one of us do God's will in regard to an unselfish practice of true Christianity as we respond to these critical issues. May we be children of God who are on the cutting edge of our faith.

H. C. BROWN, JR.

CHAPTER 1

DEATH BY EXECUTION

G. Ray Worley

The hum of the dynamo signals the prisoners on death row that the time is not far off. As he walks along the row, the chaplain observes the men who are also awaiting their "date" with the chair. Each seems on edge. One fingers a Bible. Another draws a glass of water at the sink. Still another sits on the edge of the bunk, seemingly ready to spring into action—with nowhere to go. Several men stand at the bars of their cell door, as if expecting some word or hoping for something to break the mounting tension of the evening.

Finally, the chaplain stops before one cell. It is Charles's date with the chair tonight.

What does a chaplain say to a condemned prisoner? What kinds of questions does a condemned prisoner ask? What is the role of a Christian minister to a man about to be executed?

It seems absurd, in retrospect, but small talk is easiest.

"How are you tonight, Charles?"

"Doing fine, Chaplain."

Charles is different, now, at 10:30 P.M. The top of his head is shaved. The head electrode will be placed there so that the current will flow through it into his brain. The circled fringe of hair, in a halo effect, indicates that the executioners will have no problem tonight.

Scanning his attire for Charles's date with death, the chaplain notices that the pants legs of the white prison garb have been slit. An electrode will be placed on his leg, too. Death should come quickly. A little sickening to the observer, yes. But quickly.

13

How long will a man shot through with 1,800 volts of electricity retain his consciousness? One second, two, three, five? Can the brain, violently seared with electric current, register feeling? Probably not? Will the electric current stun and disrupt all feeling? Observers believe yes.

Time is a factor. The hands of the prison clock press forward, onward, around, upward, to the point where the minute hand will mesh with the hour hand, and the booming chime of the clock will announce to the world that it is twelve o'clock. Midnight — the time of execution.

Still, the small talk.

"Is there any hope for a stay, Charles?"

"Don't know, Chaplain. Don't believe so. My lawyers appealed the case to the higher courts and the Supreme Court turned them down."

That seems to exhaust that subject. The chaplain mentally recalls the case. Charles is an average-looking Negro. He was drunk one night. A white man started to give him a hard time. Before Charles knew what had happened, the white man lay mortally wounded. Charles ran. He was caught in New Mexico. Authorities assured him that he would have little trouble in securing a manslaughter charge, so Charles obligingly signed the extradition papers permitting Texas authorities to return him to the little town where the crime was committed.

The case was typical. A court-appointed attorney argued the points of the law perfunctorily but with little enthusiasm. After all, the fee for a court-appointed case does not merit much time or effort. And the case was unpopular in the community. Sentiment was strong against Charles. An attorney must consider making a living in a small town. If he defended Charles too strongly, especially if he were successful in securing anything less than a conviction and a harsh sentence, his business would suffer. Minority races are notoriously poor in paying; the risk is not worth it. However, an oath is an oath. But attorneys pay lip service to oaths, even if a man's life is at stake.

However, chaplains are not supposed to think about community sentiment or law or justice when talking with a condemned man. The chaplain's business is to save men's souls, or so one legislator told the chaplain when he appeared before the House Committee on Criminal Jurisprudence, testifying in behalf of a bill to abolish capital punishment. The laughter of the assembled group filled the chamber as the chaplain responded to the Bible-believing and witness-baiting representative: "Sir, if you can distinguish between a man's body and his soul, I'll be indebted to you."

A man's soul. In a few short moments a soul will be knocking at the gate which popular folklore says St. Peter tends. The broad nose, the thick expanding lips, the kinky hair, the dark skin — Charles's race itself elicits the question derisively asked by a white supremist: "Do niggers have souls?"

"Do you have any favorite verses or Scripture stories you would like for me to read tonight, Charles?"

Yes, Charles remembers one or two. The psalm that begins "The Lord is my shepherd." Tonight the words, "the valley of the shadow of death," assume new meaning. Just down the corrider—a one-way corridor for Charles—is the green door. Even now a faint sound echoes from the chamber behind the green door as men test the equipment for the evening's ordeal. In contrast with that of the Psalmist, Charles's valley is smooth concrete with worn gray paint. On one side are the prison cells; on the other are windows covered by bars, which permit a glimpse of the sky, sun, and clouds by day, and the lights of other prison buildings by night. Instead of a gurgling brook, the brush of the wind upon the branches, the twitter of birds on the wing, or the rustle of scurrying animals in the brush, in Charles's "valley" there are footfalls of human beings, noises and coughs of the other condemned men, muffled conversations of the prison officials, and in the background the ominous sound of the striking clock. First the quarter, then the half, and now the three-quarter hour. The sound booms over the prison compound and filters through to where Charles sits, waiting. These are the sounds in Charles's "valley of the shadow."

Another Scripture passage? Yes, John 14. Those wonderful words that have brought comfort to many as they gazed upon the casket of a loved one or heard the minister intone Christ's promises of comfort for the living who mourn the dead. Tonight is ment of destruction—the means of wreaking corporate vengeance on a condemned man.

The ritual now dictates every action. The death decree is read and the words ring out with evil omen—"until you are dead." Customarily, the chaplain is then called upon to pronounce one last word of hope or solace. Tonight, however, this rite is forestalled by Charles's action. For when the warden asks him if he has any last word, he astonishes those present by asking to pray.

As Charles prays, the words pour forth in unlettered speech. Words of petition for care of his fellow-condemned, of appreciation for the kind treatment he has received from the guards and warden, words seeking forgiveness and asking God's blessing upon all assembled. Attendants hardened by former experiences are startled. This is the first time they have ever been prayed for by one they are to execute.

During his prayer Charles stands just inside the door, some six to eight feet from the chair. Now he is directed to sit down. The rest of the ritual is dispatched quickly. The switch is thrown and "justice" is vindicated.

A REACTION

What does a minister feel who witnesses an execution? Can he express thoughts and voice feelings?

The primary reaction to the experience is one of shock. Human life is snuffed out. That which Christians are taught to respect as sacred—human personality—is destroyed. Initially the feeling is one of unreality, as if at any moment the wardens, whom the chaplains have come to know personally, will step forward and say, "Stop!" It cannot be real. Surely this person who is living will not be killed. Not in Christian America! This seems to violate all that seminarians are taught: life, hope, faith, the gospel, redemption for sinful man.

But the warden does not say, "Stop." It is real. And Charles is dead. The chaplain feels nauseated. And fresh air is good. And the night is black. And the tension of the moment is broken. But the chaplain will never again be the same.

It is not death itself. Of course one is never fully ready for death, no matter how trained, experienced, or conditioned. Particularly when it involves a loved one or people whom one knows personally. Death of the aged, one stricken by disease, or the victim of an accident—these deaths can in some measure be accepted.

But what of this violent death? Particularly since it is prescribed as the answer for other violent deaths. Oh, this is not to forget the victim. Charles killed. He was drunk. He was somewhat primitive in spite of growing up in Christian America. At least there is some reason and explanation for his crime. But what of this?

Yes, men talk about believing the Bible. Men say they love God and hate sin. Men pray long prayers, and their voices waft heavenward as if the rising pitch of the voice carries the prayer higher, more quickly to the throne of God. Yes, men—even preachers — say capital punishment is God's will. But is it?

"Thou shalt not kill." God spoke through Moses, but to a primitive people. In so doing, He curtailed the excess of their practice of inflicting vengeance unto death for any reason. Moses stated that vengeance was to be limited, "an eye for an eye, and a tooth for a tooth." Later the prophets stated and the New Testament writers stressed, "Vengeance is mine, I will repay, saith the Lord." Jesus spoke of love, forgiveness, going the second mile, turning the other cheek, loving one's enemies — principles that burst upon the legalistic minds of the religionists of His day with the force of a great eruption from a billowing volcano. His teaching penetrated shabby lives and pricked selfish hearts with such devastating force that they could bear it no longer — they had to crucify him and find release from the guilt that his truth thrust upon them.

Men have not changed. They do not understand His message of love. Rather, they are of the same nature as the Pharisees, who sought to observe the letter of the law and neglected the spirit, who aped the form of godliness but denied the power thereof. In perfect analogy with our own day, they cloaked their lecherous hearts and their intent to defy God's Spirit by hiding behind the machinery of the state—Roman law. Ironically, they permitted

Jesus to become the victim of the capital punishment of His day
—crucifixion on the cross of Calvary. Suspended between two
thieves, He suffered the insults and blasphemy of men before His
human life ebbed away. As the piercing nails gouged out His
life upon the cross, He gazed upon the garbage dump of Jerusalem,
where the stench of the refuse and the ignominy of the location
bore witness to sinful man's continuing contempt for God.

Capital punishment today? Yes, for those who are blind . . .
spiritually. The message of God's love has opened another door
for those who see.

CHAPTER 2

THE NEW MORALITY

John A. Redhead, Jr.

"Love is the fulfilling of the law." (Romans 13:10)

George W. Cornell wrote a series of articles in the daily papers about the winds of change that are blowing through the churches. One of these is the "new theology;" another is the "new morality."

I

The best way to understand the meaning of the new morality is to see it against the background of other methods of making moral decisions.

The first is called the *legalistic*. This means that the individual gives allegiance to certain laws which provide directives for him in making decisions. If you work in a store and make a sale and you are tempted to pocket the money instead of putting it in the cash register, you remember the words, "Thou shalt not steal;" that settles the matter. If you have a date and your temptation is to let your passions go, you remember the admonition, "Thou shalt not commit adultery," and your decision is made. The *legalistic* approach recognizes an absolute standard of behavior which has been written down in a set of laws.

You will see immediately that such is the method which has been followed traditionally by the religious groups with which we are most familiar. The Jews have the Mosaic law as their guide, and Roman Catholics and Protestants have the Scriptural law. One question in the Presbyterian catechism is, "What does the Bible principally teach?" and the answer is, "The Bible principally teaches what man is to believe concerning God, and what duty God requires of man."

Actually, these two things are closely related. For example, in the Library of Congress there is a copy of the Constitution with the letters so shaded that, seen from a distance, it looks like the face of George Washington. So it is with divine law. It is a revelation of the character of God, and on that basis the believer takes it as his guide in making moral decisions.

In addition to the legalistic approach, there is the *antinomian*. The second part of the word comes from a Greek word *nomos,* which means law; the first part, *anti,* means against. It simply means "against law;" so the antinomian is the person who makes moral decisions without regard to laws or rules or principles. This man does not wish to be bothered by a set of regulations which he considers offensive and oppressive. He demands a freedom which has no regard for limiting laws.

You find something of this in the New Testament. Many of the early Christians were Jews. Their lives were regulated by laws, both moral and ceremonial. When the gospel came along to tell them that they were saved by the grace of God, not by obedience to this and that law, it brought a new kind of freedom. But some of these people got the wrong impression. They thought that laws no longer applied to Christians; and that, with their ultimate fate assured, it didn't matter what they did. This explains the warning in the First Letter of Peter. "Live as free men," he writes to them, "yet without using your freedom as a pretext for evil; but live as servants of God."

The legalist makes his moral decisions on the basis of a given law. At the opposite extreme is the antinomian, who is against all law. In between is the third approach, that of the *situationist.* He respects the ethical rules which he has inherited, but he is prepared to compromise them or "set them aside in the situation if Christian love seems better served by doing so." This is what is called situation ethics or the new morality.

In the book entitled *Situation Ethics,* the author tells a story to illustrate his theme. He says that a friend of his arrived in St. Louis at the end of a presidential campaign and his cab driver was full of talk about it. He volunteered the information that his folks for generations had been strait-jacket Republicans, which led his passenger to ask if he were going to vote Republican in the election. "No," said the driver, "there are times when a man has to push his principles aside and do the right thing." "That St. Louis cabbie," says the author, "is this book's hero."[1]

In further explanation of his position, the author elaborated his views in a newspaper interview. He said he would amend the Ten Commandments to read this way: "Thou shalt not covet— ordinarily . . . A situationist is prepared in any concrete case to suspend, ignore, or violate any principle if by doing so he can effect more good than bad by following it."

This then is the form of new morality called situation ethics. If you were called upon to size it up in the light of your understanding of our Christian faith, what would you say?

II

The first thing you can say is something that is positive. The basic point of situation ethics is well taken: one must consider what is good for persons, rather than trample on them in the name of the "law," which may actually mask an indifference, or hostility, to persons.

It is plain that such was the position of Jesus. A friend of mine wanted to play golf on Sunday afternoon, but his wife had been brought up in the old Presbyterian tradition and her conscience told her it was wrong for a church elder to engage in a pastime that was a work of neither "necessity" nor "mercy." Her husband respected her views so he suggested that they read the gospels to see if they could come to some understanding. "Do you know," he told me later, "we found that most of the passages which mentioned the sabbath told of the times when Jesus broke the law."

And that is just about the truth. In Capernaum Jesus broke the law by healing a man on the sabbath who had a withered hand. On another occasion He permitted His followers to gather

_____

[1] Joseph Fletcher, *Situation Ethics* (Philadelphia: Westminster Press, 1966)

grain on the sabbath, which was against the law. More than that, He commended David, who, when he was hungry, entered the house of worship, took the shewbread from the altar, and ate it. In Jesus' day the religious law governing the sabbath was a set of prohibitions which made the day a burden to the people, and so He laid down a principle for breaking such laws. The sabbath was made for man, He said, and not man for the sabbath. Jesus insisted that the good of persons was the supreme good and any law which contradicted that was secondary. In that sense the new morality has a point.

III

But in Romans 13:10 Paul says, "Love is the fulfilling of the law."

In the twelfth chapter of Romans, Paul started to talk about Christian behavior, and in the thirteenth chapter he began to be specific. "Owe no one anything except to love one another," he said. This is a favorite text with supporters of the new morality. Paul gave four of the social commandments: the commandments against stealing, killing, committing adultery, and coveting. And then he said: "Love does no wrong to a neighbor; therefore love is the fulfilling of the law." (RSV)

There are two senses in which you can fulfill something. The first is to complete it and bring it to consummation so that it comes to an end. Christians have sometimes been tempted to think about the fulfillment of the law in that sense: Christian love is the end of the law. That is, once you are in Christ you are beyond the law, and the ordinary ground rules do not apply to you anymore. Let your conscience be your guide, and love your rule of life.

But you can also fulfill something in the sense that you carry it out to completion. You do not put an end to it, because you cannot fulfill something unless you have it to begin with. You cannot fulfill the law of God unless the law is there to be carried out. Paul did not say, "Love does away with the law." He said, "Love fulfills the law." And that seems to be the point of view of Jesus, for He said once: "Think not that I am come to destroy the law, or the prophets: I am not come to destroy but to fulfill."

I believe that the new morality is inadequate on two counts. The first is that it gives up the guidance which comes from a moral absolute and gets lost in a sea of relativity. Dr. David Read of New York says that a friend of his was once speaking to a group of students in England about the absolute claim of God on our lives. When the question period began, one student protested that there were no absolutes at all. "Everything is relative; nothing can be absolute." The speaker asked if he were sure of what he was saying. "Yes," he said, "I'm sure." "Are you *absolutely* sure?" "Yes," he said—then realized he had fallen into a trap. But this isn't just a trick of language. All that is worthwhile in human civilization has to do with a sense of the absolute—the very highest against which all our efforts are measured. You cannot say that one course of conduct is relatively better than another unless there is some absolute against which you are measuring them. "Better" makes sense only in the light of "best."

Suppose you change the Seventh Commandment to read, "Thou shalt not commit adultery—ordinarily." Where is the person of omniscient mind who knows enough to change the law of God? Suppose you say with Dr. Joseph Fletcher: "A situationist would discard all absolutes except the one absolute: always to act with loving concern." But how does one know what love means? The new morality seems to forget that the moral law of God has served to save us from the mistakes of a trial and error system of ethics, and that the "thou shalts" and "thou shalt nots" have gone a long way toward helping us to know what is good and what is bad for persons in certain situations.

The situationist says there is but one law, concern for the good of the other person, but Jesus says there are two. Love God; and then you know how to love your neighbor. You cannot let love of neighbor be your guide until you have made the law of God your rule.

There is a practice of the insurance companies for which I am grateful. When you buy a policy there is a date on which payment of your premium is due, but there is a grace period. The law says that payment is due on a particular date, but the company will accept payment anytime within the thirty-day period. Without the law there would not be any grace.

There is a second point in which the new morality is inadequate: It fails to take into account the nature of human nature.

If people were perfect and could always be trusted to base their behavior on what is good for others, the new morality would make more sense. But this world is not such a fool's paradise. Do away with the laws which define the demands of love, and some other principle will rush in to determine conduct. Self-love— whether in the form of lying, cheating, stealing, killing, or promiscuity between the sexes will fill the vacuum left by an explicit law.

A certain man was asked by his priest why he had not been to confession, and he replied that he had heard they were going to do away with the Ten Commandments. Any such report is likely, for some time to come, to be highly exaggerated. God has not repealed the Commandments and there is little chance that He will. Paul says love is the fulfilling, but not the end, of the law.

In the Gospel there is the beautiful story of Jesus and the woman taken in adultery. By way of contrast with the treatment of her accusers our Lord forgave her. The thing we are likely to remember about this story is His tenderness and compassion. It is a standing rebuke to the harsh judgment of which some religious people can be guilty. But this is not all that Jesus did. He said, "Neither do I condemn thee. Go, and sin no more." With these three words He reaffirmed the moral law—the validity of the absolute standard.

It is our task always to have understanding and to show compassion, but in a time of lawlessness such as ours, it makes more sense to affirm the standards of morality than to discuss the exceptions.

CHAPTER 3

THE CHRISTIAN MEANING OF SEX

Gordon Clinard

From the Playboy Club in Chicago to the Vatican in Rome, sex oozes out of the pores of our culture. From Hefner to Robinson and Fletcher, it is a vital facet of the new morality which, in the name of freedom and of love, tells us that ethics are totally situational. Called by one theologian the "last frontier," sex has become in the last decades the god with which our culture is preoccupied. We are saddled with a kind of adolescent fantasy, a profusion of pornography which men in particular ogle in offices, clubs, restaurants, and locker rooms. Topless waitresses are now declared to be a psychological and healthy corrective for the bosom fantasy with which the American male has been preoccupied for decades.

This exploitation of sex is not new. If there is anything new about it, it is the theological sanction which it currently receives. Hefner and his Playboy devotees are not new—but Robinson and Fletcher, the theologians, at least attempt to be. In the words of Joseph Fletcher, they come to every moral decision, including the sexual decision, "armed with the ethical maxims of the community and its heritage" which are treated with "respect as illuminators of problems: but which they are prepared to compromise or set aside in the situation if love seems better served by doing so."[1] No one can deny that we are caught up in a moral revolution which, whether in the "sleep-ins" of the anti-God worship of sex or in the intellectual circles of situation ethics, poses a challenge to the family as the basic unit of our society.

---

[1] *Situation Ethics* (Philadephia: The Westminster Press, 1966), p. 26.

27

We are all involved in this matter. After a group of Catholic priests had voted, by about a 60 percent majority, in favor of freedom from the vow of celibacy, the *Catholic News Magazine* carrying the story punctuated its meaning with an enlightening cartoon. An aging and rotund priest was pictured saying to himself, "Thank God I am not like that 60%." Well, only old age saves any one of us from the problems of sex, for we are all sexual creatures. Furthermore, this moral revolution affects all of us at the point of our families; there is hardly a family which has not been touched directly or indirectly by it.

The moral revolution is not the only sexual threat to family life. We all know how central all sexual behavior is to family well-being. Sex is invariably involved in marriage difficulties. It may be because of some sexual aberration or inadequacy, psychological or physical. More often, however, other problems in the marriage create difficulty in the sexual relationship.

So central is sex to the well-being of the home that improper teaching and example on the part of parents create inevitable difficulties in the marriages of their children. A young man and his wife of a few months went to his pastor to discuss the problems which threatened to end their marriage in divorce. It developed that he never knew his parents to display any affection for one another before the children. Furthermore, they never gave him any instruction in sex. He grew up with the idea that sex was something you didn't talk about. Since he never heard a sermon on the subject, he felt that sex was something not really "nice." It was on the border of sin, if not sin itself.

To complicate matters, he once had been in love with a young lady for whom he had no sexual feelings—she was his ideal of womanhood, the perfect one, and physical attraction was not a part of that adoration. He felt differently about the girl he married. In fact he had had sex with her before marriage. After marriage he was overcome by guilt because of his premarital relationship with her and because of the way he felt about sex in general. The image of the first love without sex kept haunting him. So his marriage was a failure.

A proper understanding of sex is essential to a solid and Christian marriage, and I believe it is time for the church to speak out on the Christian meaning of sex. One of our most serious problems in this total picture is the silence of our churches on the subject. It is time for us to communicate a Biblical theology of sex. What meaning does the biblical revelation give to sex?

SEX AND PERSONHOOD—A FREEDOM

Sex is a part of the doctrine of creation. It is a part of what it is to be a person. The sex drive is a gift from God. As Jesus said, "He which made them at the beginning made them male and female" (Matt. 19:4).

When we retrace our steps to Genesis, we encounter the truth that woman was made for man so that he might be a complete person. She was a help "meet" for him. In her, man found his fulfillment. And, in turn, she found her true person completed in him. There can be no doubt that the sexual relation is at the heart of this fulfillment of personhood, for the words of Genesis 2:24 make it clear enough: "Therefore shall a man leave his father and his mother, and shall cleave unto his wife: and they shall be one flesh." Man does not truly exist except in relationship—he finds himself in his relation to others. So sex is a vital part of personhood. No wonder the Bible speaks of the sexual relation as "knowing." Jesus sanctioned the same teaching by quoting the Genesis verse and adding, "Wherefore they are no more twain, but one flesh."

This is where the Christian meaning of sex begins. Sex is a gift of God intended for man's completion as a person. There are several vital implications of this fact.

The most obvious is that there is nothing sinful about sex. The idea that sex was the original sin cannot be substantiated in the Bible. Not even in I Corinthians 7, in which the gift of celibacy is exalted, is there any suggestion that the sexual drive is sinful. The original sin of man was his proud effort to be God. His refusal to be a creature, his pride, his rebellion against God—these form the basic sin of Adam as first man and of Adam as Everyman.

This sin affected sex as it affected all other phases of man's personality. Dr. John Howell has stated that result well—sin has resulted in shame, exploitation, and lust.[2] The first chapter of Romans pictures not the sinfulness of sex but the sordidness of sex perverted by sin. So sex is God-given. It is for the good of man. It is intended for his completion as a person. It is right that the Genesis writer concluded his account of creation, which included the creation of man as male and female, with the word, "And God saw every thing that he had made, and, behold, it was very good" (Gen. 1:31).

Such an understanding of sex lifts its purpose out of the area of procreation only. Obviously, the sex drive has been given to man as a part of his power to create life after the image of God. But there is no Biblical evidence that sex was meant only for the purpose of reproduction. Sex is for the purpose of fulfillment of the person. Certainly Paul could not have had procreation in mind, primarily, when he urged upon Christian husbands and wives that they not refrain from sexual relations except for brief periods of time agreed upon by mutual consent for purposes of special devotion to God (I Cor. 7:3-5). Theologians such as Augustine, who have argued that any sexual relation in marriage except for the purpose of begetting children is sinful, have no real Biblical evidence on which to stand. Any adequate position on birth control and family responsibility must be built on the Christian meaning of sex as the completion of personhood.

Another vital implication of this doctrine of sex as the fulfillment of human personhood is that the entire person is involved in the sexual relationship. The Greek concept that man can be divided into spirit and body, the idea that the flesh is the focal point of evil, the feeling that one can indulge the flesh without involving the spirit—these are unknown to the Hebrew-Christian doctrine of man. Paul used the term "flesh," not to mean that sin finds its origin in the physical flesh but in the sense that sin finds one of its prime means of entering the personality through the appetites of the body. When he used the term "flesh," he referred to the unredeemed personality of man—man in his carnal, unre-

---

[2] *Teaching About Sex* (Nashville: Broadman Press, 1966), pp. 24-27.

deemed state. In relation to sin, the "word flesh has lost its physical meaning and has acquired an ethical meaning."[3]

Since all sin involves the person, the entire man is affected by sin. But sexual sin especially involves man as a total person. Because sex is given of God for the completion of personhood, it is by the sexual act that one is "joined" to another in a unique way. Thus Paul mentioned, in I Corinthians 6:15-18, a unique result of sexual sin on man's personhood. This sin, above all others, has a total and lasting effect upon man as a person. In illicit sex "the interpersonal relationship has undergone a radical change, and the couple involved can never return to where they were before."[4] Even with a prostitute, sex means a "joining," a becoming of one flesh. There is no such thing as casual sex, because sex is so uniquely related to man as person.

Thus, sex, meant for the completion of man as a person, is one of our great freedoms as persons. The new moralists speak much of freedom—sexual freedom is a gift from God, indeed— but let them understand what freedom means. God's laws on sexual behavior are not arbitrary laws designed by a capricious God; none of God's laws are. They are ground rules for freedom. The only thing wrong with adultery is that it is not the way. The only thing wrong with fornication is that it is not the way. The only thing wrong with homosexuality is that it is not the way. He which made them at the beginning made them male and female, and said, "For this cause shall a man leave his father and mother, and shall cleave to his wife: and they two shall be one flesh." This is the freedom of one of God's great and good gifts—sex is the completion of personhood.

SEX AND LOVE—A FULFILLMENT

Those who justify a relative ethic on sex do so in the name of love. As Bishop Robinson wrote, "Nothing can of itself be labelled as 'wrong.' One cannot, for instance, start from the posi-

3William Barclay, *The Mind of St. Paul* (New York: Harper and Brothers, 1958), p. 198.
4William Graham Cole, *Sex and Love in the Bible* (New York: Associated Press, 1959), p. 254.

tion 'sex relations before marriage' or 'divorce' are wrong or sinful in themselves. They may be in 99 cases or even 100 cases out of 100, but they are not intrinsically so, for the only intrinsic evil is lack of love."[5] Admittedly, this radical ethic of the situation, with nothing prescribed except love, sounds appealing. It sounds strangely like the Christian's freedom from the law to live his life in all of his relationships on the "royal law" of love. One can scarcely find a better summary of the meaning of Christian love, *agape,* than found in Joseph Fletcher's book, *Situation Ethics* (see especially pp. 57ff).

But one wonders if this definition of love knows the Christian meaning of the term. It should be emphasized that the Christian meaning of sex is found in love. Sex and love are not to be equated, but sex is a profound expression of love at its deepest level. So it is in love that the sexual relationship finds its fulfillment.

No Biblical passage makes this clearer than Ephesians 5: 22-23. Wives are admonished to be subordinate to their husbands in everything on the premise that husbands are worthy of their confidence and trust. Love is the basis for such a relationship, for husbands are enjoined to keep on loving their wives, as Christ loved the church and gave Himself for it. The qualities of *agape* love are dramatically pictured in this passage: It is an outgoing, selfless love. It is a love which is primarily concerned about others. It is a love whose first question is never, "What is to my best interest?" The first question is always, "What is to your best interest?" That Paul includes the sexual relation in this passage is made certain by the "one flesh" concept which is central to it. The passage speaks in majestic terms which make the concept of marriage and its relationship in love akin to the mysterious oneness of Christ and His church. "It is a relationship in which man and wife come to be so closely related one to the other that they can in full truth be spoken of as one. It is this very relationship which makes for the appropriate expression of their mutual responsibilities."[6]

    [5]John A. T. Robinson, *Honest to God* (Philadelphia: The Westminster Press, 1963), p. 118.
    [6]Ray Summers, *Pattern for Christian Living* (Nashville: Broadman Press, 1960), p. 126.

When sex is an expression of this kind of love, it is exalted into something rich and beautiful. It is the beginning, consummating, and continuing expression of love in marriage. Such love, the only emotion which distinguishes sex from lust and lifts it above biological release of tension, can never permit the sexual partner to be an object. One of the critics of Hugh Hefner's "Playboy philosophy" has struck a precise blow at the misinterpretation of love which characterizes the new morality: "There is the implicit premise that woman is an object. She has no other function than to be lusted after and lurched at."[7] It should be noted that the lust which reduces sex to a selfish use of another's body as an object can exist in marriage as well as outside marriage. Only *agape* love is a proper basis for marriage and for the sexual relations which consummate and continue it.

The Christian view of sex is that it is a sublime expression of divine-like love in marriage. New Testament reference to sex in its intended purpose comes within the environment of marriage. Outside of marriage sex can hardly express *agape* love; it may express "I love me, and I want you." It may express, "We love each other, and we shall ignore the hurt we shall possibly do to innocents." But it cannot express *agape* love for all involved. It is at this very point of concern for the other that the Christian view of sex is, in my judgment, at variance with the precepts of the new morality. Any expression of love which is the pursuit of one's own pleasure or the pleasure of two with disregard for the needs and emotions of other people falls short of the *agape* love of which sex should be an expression. It begins in self-love and ends in lovelessness. But in Christian married love the loved one is loved for his or her own sake, for his or her own worth.

Here is the love of which sex is the proper fulfillment:

I love you, not only for what you are, but for what I am when I am with you.

I love you not only for what you have made of yourself but for what you are making of me.

I love you for the part of me you bring out.

7"Think Clean," *Time* (March 3, 1967), p. 80.
Press, 1960), p. 126.

I love you for putting your hand into my heaped-up heart and passing over all the foolish, weak things that you can't help seeing there, and for drawing out into the light all the beautiful things that no one else had looked quite far enough to find.

I love you for ignoring the possibility of the fool and weakling in me and for laying firm hold on the good in me.

I love you for not seeing the glaring ugliness in me and for multiplying the beauties by the admiration of them.

I love you because you are helping me to make of the lumber of my life not a tavern but a temple—out of the works of my every day not a reproach but a song.

I love you because you have done more than any creed could have done to make me good and more than any fate could have done to make me happy.

Love is very patient, very kind.

Loves knows no jealousy; love makes no parade, gives itself no airs, is never rude, never selfish, never irritated, never resentful; love is never glad when others go wrong, love is gladdened by goodness, always slow to expose, always eager to believe the best, always hopeful, always patient.

Love never disappears.

SEX AND THE LORDSHIP OF CHRIST—A COMMITMENT

The Christian meaning of sex finds its climax, as does every other facet of life for the child of God, in the lordship of Christ. There is another option on sex than those proposed by the new moralists—another besides legalism, antinomianism, and situationism. It is the option of Christian liberty.

Our secular culture calls for something better for the Christian solution to sex than legalism could ever offer. As someone put it rather humorously, "the three deterrents to free sex have been fear of pregnancy, fear of disease, fear of detection. These have now been eliminated by the pill, penicillin, and privacy." What can restrain men today? I have a suggestion—the lordship of Christ. The belief that Christ is the master of all of my life— in the bedroom as well as in the office, on a business trip as well as on the family vacation. The idea that my body is sacred, that it is the temple of the Holy Spirit, and that I am to offer it as a "living sacrifice, holy, acceptable unto God, which is your reasonable service." A full commitment to Christ—a practice of God's will in all of life—this is our restraint and this is our freedom. And it is the commitment which gives the highest meaning to sex. In the words of Dwight Small, "When a Christian couple experience the power of His love over their life together, then in their love for Him they will find their own. Their love for Christ is the bond of their oneness, the growing strength and quality of their love for each other."[8]

What then should we do as pastors and Christian leaders with regard to the propagation of a Christian view of sex as a vital part of responsible family life?

(1) Let us for ourselves, and in so far as possible for others, build Christian homes. Let us do all we can to build strong Christian marriages where love is obvious, where morality is practiced and taught, where healthy sex education begins, and where children grow up in the atmosphere of affection for one another and the devotion of all of life to Christ. This helps to build a Christian view of sex.

(2) Let us do more preaching and teaching on sex. Let us make it clear that the sex drive is sacred and that the Christian has a responsibility to accept the lordship of Christ for every relation of life. Let us challenge contemporary Christians to personal moral integrity.

(3) Let us exert our influence for social morality. The smut rakers should know that we are in the world. The movie and television industries should be touched by our constructive effort to preserve the Hebrew-Christian ethic of sexual morality. We should be in the forefront of community leadership in proper sex education.

(4) We should practice forgiveness. We minister to hundreds who have fallen into the vices of sexual immorality. Indeed, if the Sermon on the Mount is correct, we minister to no one

8Dwight H. Small, *Design for Christian Marriage* (Westwood, New Jersey: Fleming H. Revell Company, 1959), p. 70.

who has not. But the fallen ones known to society are at our doorsteps. Jesus knew how to love the sinner while loathing his sin. We, too, must offer the hope of new life in Christ.

CHAPTER 4

SEX: A CRUCIAL ISSUE FOR CHRISTIAN AMERICANS

Thomas A. Bland

Sex is as old as man's creation by God. Sex is as new as the shared life of this very day. Sex is variously regarded as a blessing and a curse, as liberating and enslaving, as fulfilling and depriving. There is an element of partial truth in each of the preceding paradoxical statements about that basic fact of human nature called "sex."

Mankind has, during the long years of human history, sought ways to relate sex to the totality of life. One way has been the exploitation of sexual powers. Radical denial and repression of sexuality have been other negative responses. For the greater part, when man has allowed his patterns of life to be enlightened by religious truth, he has known that sexuality is related to God and to the whole fabric of human relations in the light of his knowledge of God. As a reading of both the Old and New Testaments will reveal, the nature and purposes of human sexuality are matters of religious concern.

Christian faith accepts God's creation of man as male and female as a good act. Sex, therefore, is a gift. Since it is from God, it is essentially a good gift. One's existence as male or female is a reality which is to be gratefully accepted. The purposes to which the unique sexual powers of male or female are directed should be in keeping with, not contrary to, the will of God. One of the concerns of this chapter is to state these purposes. Before doing so, however, we need to state some evidences of the urgency of Christian answers to sexual expressions in the contemporary American scene.

We Americans are living in a society which is saturated
with sexual stimuli. Sexual symbols are employed by advertisers
to sell products ranging from toothpaste to automobiles and household furnishings. Popular literature, from the short story to the
novel, is filled with all kinds of sex, some of it wholesome and
normal, some of it perverted and ghastly. The performing arts,
through the media of stage, screen, and television, exploit the
basic human and social interests in sex in dramatizing life in our
times. But before issuing a broadside barrage of criticism against
persons in the fields of advertising, writing, and performing, we
must remember that these media reflect, as well as create, the interests of society.

Other social factors which are prevalent in the late twentieth
century add to the current explosion of sexual problems. Greater
freedom of association between young people has been made possible by the automobile, the motel, the coeducational residential
college, and the relaxation of family and community controls.
None of these things are, in themselves, good or bad. But it cannot be denied that they provide the settings for greater freedom of
choice on the part of young people with regard to patterns of
dating and courtship and the option of premarital sexual intercourse.

Technological advances in contraception, especially in the
effectiveness of the "pill," have diminished whatever deterrent
value there might have been in the fear of pregnancy as a dis-
couragement of premarital or extramarital sexual intercourse.
Furthermore, the ability of medical science to treat venereal
diseases has removed another factor of fear from sexual relations
outside of marriage.

It is evident that fears of detection (because of the mobility
and anonymity of life in an urban culture), of conception (because of more effective contraceptive means), and of infection
from venereal diseases (because of penicillin and other "wonder"
drugs) have largely vanished as protectors of premarital chastity.
However, despite the scientific advances in the control of human
fertility, there has been a marked increase in births out of wedlock. Currently, there are about 250,000 per year in the United
States. A 400 percent increase in infectious syphilis has occurred

within the past decade, despite advances in the medical treatment of venereal diseases. Teenagers and young adults are particularly vulnerable to hazards of births out of wedlock and syphilitic infection.

It is highly undesirable to base an appeal for responsible sexual behavior on fear. Neither fear of pregnancy or infectious syphilis nor knowledge of scientific facts of fertility control has served to deter persons from very irresponsible sexual activity. We must look closer for causes.

I

Behavior always reflects values. If we are to learn what is causing the contemporary sexual revolution in American society, we must try to discover some of the changing values which bear upon these patterns of life.

One crucial change in values pertaining to sexual behavior centers in naturalistic assumptions about sex. Biology and Christian faith have no quarrel with the claim that sex is natural. A healthy sexual appetite is as normal as a healthy appetite for food. Biologically, the human organism is motivated by normal drives, including hunger and sex. But an intelligent person does not satisfy his hunger drive without consideration of the edibility, sanitation, and preparation of food. The hunger drive is not satisfied by a normal person without making value judgments. Likewise, the wonderful, God-given sexual drive is not to be satisfied without regard for values. Sexual expression in humans is potentially as far above a merely animal level of expression as human speech is superior to noises made by animals in communication.

Three false assumptions undergird a naturalistic value structure of sex: (1) The assumption that, as a natural thing, sex is automatically self-fulfilling is grossly erroneous. Sexual expression, to be really meaningful, must be fulfilled in the context of other basic human relationships. (2) The assumption that one must have sex or get sick is undoubtedly used as an excuse for sexual license. However, the expression of sex without regard to other values can lead to serious emotional illnesses. (3) The assumption that sex can be treated casually fails to take account of the deep interpersonal, social consequences of sexual acts. When these acts are irresponsible, great harm can follow. A naturalistic view of sex is therefore subhuman, irresponsible, and demonic.

A second set of values on which much contemporary sexual behavior is based is hedonism. Hedonism holds that one should do the things that bring pleasure. It cannot be denied that sexual experience is pleasurable (and is designed by God for responsible enjoyment). If pleasure is elevated to become the highest value, selfish gratification is the goal of sexual activity.

The most outspoken exposition of thoroughgoing hedonism in sex is to be found in the Playboy philosophy of Hugh Hefner, whose magazine *Playboy* has a circulation of over three million. Hefner's magazine, and his related network of men's clubs, complete with "bunny" girls, has made him the principal owner of a fifty-million-dollar empire. According to the Playboy philosophy, sex is for enjoyment, especially for males. This philosophy holds that there is nothing wrong with premarital sexual intercourse provided no element of coercion is involved. Between consenting partners sex "for fun," without such entangling alliances as abiding love and marriage, is readily permissible. Hefner's editorials are very critical of traditional Christian views of sexuality. Hefner sees classical Christianity from Paul through Calvin to modern church teaching as antisexual. The hedonistic Playboy philosophy views sexual freedom in the same category as freedom of speech. In short, one's sexual activity is his own business. Attempts by society or religion to impose controls is to interfere with personal freedom.

The hedonistic philosophy of *Playboy* is particularly alluring to persons who may be looking for an excuse for sexual expression without restraints. It is especially appealing to college-age young people, many of whom are enjoying for the first time in their lives the "heady wine" of freedom from home and parents. Unfortunately, these young people frequently do not possess the objectivity and maturity to see the fatal flaws in the Playboy philosophy.

Three serious criticisms, at least, can be leveled at the hedonistic view of sex. (1) This view sees the meaning of masculinity in terms of sexual prowess. To the immature teen-ager or young adult male, it offers the grossly false claim that manhood and aggressive sexual fulfillment are synonymous. (2) This is an anti-feminist philosophy. The female's enjoyment of sex is considered incidental and unimportant. The female is really regarded as an object for the male's gratification. The woman is treated as a commodity, not as a person. (3) The casual recreational view of sex is misleading. Sexuality is so fundamental in human nature that fleeting, transitory, or even steady "recreational" affairs cannot be separated from the total life experiences of persons. What happens to people and between people adds up to liberation and growth or to enslavement and dwarfing of personality. Such a mistaken view of sex leads ultimately to idolatry. Therefore, the Christian faith and ethic must condemn this philosophy as a modern idolatrous paganism.

A third value system influencing sexual attitudes and behavior in our day seems to stand in rather sharp contrast to naturalism and hedonism. But in terms of actual content the contrast is not so sharp, as we shall see presently. I refer to the so-called "new morality." While naturalism and hedonism make no claims to Christian origin, the "new morality" advocates claim that its origin is Christian.

Before discussing specific teachings of the "new morality" with respect to sex, we must note that the expression, "the new morality," has a larger frame of reference than sex. Its chief claim is that when one comes to any situation calling for ethical decision, he should make his decision in the situation on the basis of one principle, and only one. That principle is love, the *agape* of the New Testament. Nothing else—no rule, no law, no Scripture text, nothing—is ultimately authoritative except love. In each situation one must decide, "What does love require?" "What is the loving thing to do?" The question is phrased in this manner because, say adherents of this viewpoint, love is a predicate, not something substantive; it is always acting, always doing.

According to this system, one cannot prejudge an act. Only in the situation can he decide and act responsibly. As Robinson has put it, nothing can be labelled "wrong" in and of itself.

One cannot, for instance, start from the position "sex relations before marriage" . . . are wrong or sinful in themselves. They may be in 99 cases or even 100 cases out of 100, but they are not intrinsically so, for the only intrinsic evil is lack of love.[1] The claim of the proponents of "the new morality" is that the only good in all circumstances is love. To act contrary to love is the greatest wrong. One comes to the decision-making moment armed with the insights, teachings, and wisdom of society, but prepared to suspend or violate any rule except to act in love for the good of his neighbor. With respect to sexual behavior, one critical reactor to this teaching observed: "Which is quite a long thought for an 18-year-old during a passionate moment in the back seat of a car."[2]

In the realm of sexual relations the "new morality" denies any absolute claim for premarital chastity. Similarly, adultery is not always wrong. Both premarital and extramarital relations, as well as marital relations, must be judged "right" or "wrong" on the sole basis of love. Consequently, the new morality's sexual ethic is permissive, privately interpreted, and adjudged on the basis of affection.

The supremacy of love (*agape*) in Christian ethics has long been recognized. Hence, when advocates of "the new morality" speak in such glowing terms of love (*agape*), a wide circle of agreement is established. When, however, the thoughtful inquirer begins to probe in order to discover what is meant by "love" as used by Robinson and Fletcher, he is confronted with second thoughts. One looks in vain for any description of the substance of love (*agape*) as found in I Corinthians 13. One is confronted with the claim that love and justice are the same. Against the New Testament understanding of *agape* as a disposition of good will, expressed in acts of recognition, consideration, and care and incarnated supremely in Jesus of Nazareth, the understanding of *agape* on the part of proponents of "the new morality" stands empty and void of substance. Further, in dealing with a human reality as powerful as sex, *agape* can easily become distorted or

---

[1]John A. T. Robinson, *Honest to God* (London: SCM Press, 1963), p. 118.
[2]*Time* (March 5, 1965), p. 44.

replaced by selfish desire or lust. Bluntly stated, "I love you" may mean, when uttered in the excitement of aroused sexual desire, "I love *me,* and I *want* you."

Another claim of "the new morality" is that it stands in a "middle-of-the-road" position between the extremes of legalism and antinomianism. On surface investigation this has great appeal. Careful probing draws out a negative response to a question such as this: "Could the commandment, 'Thou shalt not commit adultery,' be an absolute norm?" The answer "no" leads us to conclude that such an answer really means that law and love are contradictory. In contrast, the Biblical tradition in the history of Christianity has seen law was a vehicle of God's love. Law is, in fact, a method employed by the loving, sovereign God in governing a sinful world.

"The new morality," while claiming to steer clear of antinomianism, actually bogs down in the attempt. Man becomes the judge and juror of his own act in the decision-making moment. This can lead to all manner of sinful, selfish rationalization of behavior and exploitation of another person. Its claim to the contrary notwithstanding, "the new morality" is antinomian.

Applied to sexual ethics, "the new morality" is too individualistic. Sexual activity is basically social. Therefore, other persons and society at large have a right to be heard and heeded on such an important matter. Secondly, the understanding of "love" in "the new morality" is too general and naive. Especially when applied to sexual ethics, too little allowance is made for selfish expressions of love. A third criticism of "the new morality" is that the view of human nature which underlies it is unrealistic. It fails to take into account the Biblical understanding of human nature as sinful. In short, "the new morality" is a treacherous and untrustworthy value guide for sexual life.

II

In a culture shot through with values of naturalism, hedonism, and "the new morality," the intelligent Christian must construct a sex ethic which is Biblically based, Christ-centered, and consistent with the basic needs of human nature. To that task we now turn.

Man, a sexual being, was created by God for community. The basic form of community is sexual, finding expression in the social institutions of marriage and the family.

In Christian thought sex and marriage are clearly interrelated. Marriage is that form of enduring community where husband and wife may responsibly share with each other the unique powers of sex. The mystery of the otherness of the partner is basically spiritual and unfathomable. The differences between male and female are far more profound than differences in anatomy. It is in relation to this woman, my wife, that I gain unique insight into the meaning of manhood. Similarly, this woman, my wife, learns through me a unique meaning of her womanhood. It is no accident that the Bible speaks of one's marital partner as a "helpmeet." This actually means one capable of answering the other's needs, of helping the other to find fulfillment. Within marriage sexual integrity is affirmed as husband and wife live together for their individual and common good.

In the community of marriage sexual intercourse establishes and nourishes the unity of the pair. The "one flesh" spoken of in the Bible is both substance and symbol of deep union. "For this reason a man shall leave his father and mother and be joined to his wife, and the two shall become one" (Mark 10:7 RSV). Christian teaching regards the profound nature of sexual intercourse with such seriousness that it asserts that marriage ought to be permanent.

Between husband and wife sexual intercourse is a means of revelation. "Intercourse" means "communication," and in the sexual act mutual communication takes place. The Old Testament reference to intercourse as "to know" is a recognition that in this relationship "deep calleth unto deep." Humanity answers its fellow humanity; real knowing takes place!

"Love is a many splendored thing!" In marriage sexual intercourse affords an opportunity for unique communication of interpersonal love between husband and wife. There is passion, or desire. Without this elemental form of human love, there can be no sexual communication. In marriage passion is directed toward the partner. Consequently, erotic love, which places a high valuation on the partner and desires intimate fellowship with the partner, makes a contribution to marital love. At the deepest level is *agape,* that form of love which wills the good of the other.

Permanent, monogamous marriage affords the best opportunity for two human beings to fulfill their lives as sexual beings. Here man and woman can create true community. Here they can know as they are known. Here love is given and received in the context of responsibility. Marriage alone, among the various settings for sexual activity, offers a community where, day by day, for better or for worse, all the purposes of sex can be related to a total life partnership. One reason that sexual activity outside of marriage is wrong is that sex must be related to total life experience in continuing community. I agree heartily with the statement of the theologian, Karl Barth: "Coitus without coexistence is demonic."[3]

Marriage and family come together when a couple join in the procreation of offspring. Here God calls man and woman to enter into creation with Him. In classical Christian thought the procreation and education of offspring are always related. Persons who beget and bear children are normally expected to rear them. This is another reason why the sustained relationships of permanent marriage are needed as the setting in which the role of parenthood is undertaken and fulfilled.

In the light of my understanding of God's purposes and of the nature and destiny of man, I see two ways in which sexual integrity can be expressed. One of these is sexual continence outside of marriage. This allows for the choice of a celibate life, although there is no Biblical basis for putting celibacy above marriage as the Roman Catholic Church does. When celibacy is chosen as a vocation, it should be because one's own understanding of the work he will be doing under God would make this the better arrangement. In other words, celibacy is not chosen as an end in itself, but as a means to another vocational end. What about people who do not willingly choose to remain single but are forced by circumstances to do so? The disproportionate distribution of the sexes makes finding a mate virtually impossible for some people in parts of the world. Further, personal and family situations

---

[3]Karl Barth, *Church Dogmatics* (Edinburgh: T and T Clark, 1958), Vol. III, 4, p. 133.

sometimes make individuals the very unfortunate victims of un-chosen spinsterhood or bachelorhood. Whatever the circumstances, the way of sexual integrity is the life of continence.

The second way of sexual integrity is chastity within mar-riage. Fidelity to one's partner is a precondition of this way of in-tegrity. The nature of the sexual relationship is so profound that it calls for free, mutual consent between a man and a woman to live together "from this day forward, for better, for worse, for richer, for poorer, in sickness and in health." Moreover, it calls for faithful covenant making and covenant keeping between a man and a woman, a couple and society, and a couple and God.

III

In this chapter we have done two things: (1) We have de-scribed and evaluated the cultural forces and value systems which influence sexual attitudes and practices in America today. (2) We have set forth, in brief form at least, essential elements of an adequate Christian sex ethic. In seeking answers to problems con-fronting Christian Americans, I think that both emphases of this chapter are important.

Christian parents and Christian churches need to become better teachers if we are to turn the tide in the direction of more wholesome Christian sexual thinking and living. This teaching will involve imparting information, entering into real dialogue with our children and young people, and offering to children and youth an example of consistent, joyful, abundant Christian living.

CHAPTER 5

DIVORCE AMERICAN STYLE

Drew J. Gunnells, Jr.

It is a sad commentary on life in modern America that divorce is as much a part of the "American way" as the hot dog or the Coca Cola. In fact, in no other area have we achieved such dubious leadership as we have in the matter of divorce. For the past twenty years we have led all the nations of the world in the number of divorces granted. As ironic as it may seem, Christian America is far ahead of atheistic Russia at the point of broken homes. "Divorce American Style" is both frequent and damaging. Nearly one out of every four marriages today will end in the divorce court; one out of every three marriages today is a remarriage; one out of every nine children living in America today is a step child; 350,000 children every year become stepchildren as a direct result of the divorce court. The number one cause of juvenile delinquency is the broken home. I could go on and on and on!

We are all affected by the problem of divorce. In fact, I dare say there is not a family today that does not have within its confines someone who is divorced. We have friends and neighbors who are divorced. We either are or have been divorced ourselves, or we are affected by it simply because we are in the ministry of counseling and rehabilitation. In whatever way we are affected by divorce, we are all acutely aware that it is a serious problem.

Divorce is a problem which continues to arise either because we do not understand the Christian concept of marriage or because we disregard the teachings of the Bible. Here I would like to do two things: analyze what Jesus said about the problem of divorce; and apply what He said to life as we find it today.

I am aware that in spite of the tremendous problem of divorce in our society there is a lack of easily available material on the subject. I have subscribed to a leading periodical since its beginning, and in ten years of its publication I have not found one article dealing specifically with the subject of divorce. I looked back through the Adult lessons of the International Uniform Lesson Series and found that during the last five years there has not been one lesson on the Scripture passages dealing specifically with divorce. Sermonic literature dealing with the subject is just as scarce. So, contrary to what one might have thought, not much has been said or written on the subject by churchmen. "Can this marriage be saved?" is a question seemingly discussed only in the secular press. Can it be that modern conditions concerning divorce have come about, at least in part, by the church's unwillingness to face frankly and fairly the problem of divorce?

Even if the modern church has avoided the issue of divorce, the same cannot be said for Jesus Christ—the Lord of the church.

What Jesus Said About Divorce

Pharisees came to Jesus one day and asked a question about divorce: "Is it lawful for a man to put away his wife for every cause?" (Matt. 19:3). This question involved the matter of divorce and remarriage. Divorce was a disputed question in the first century just as it is today. This group of Pharisees asked Jesus for His interpretation of Deuteronomy 24:1-2. The Jews themselves had two schools of thought on the matter. Their conservatives, the school of Shammai, said that one could be divorced only for the cause of adultery. The liberal element, the school of Hillel, said "for every cause." These Pharisees were not really seeking the truth; but they wanted to involve Jesus in a theological snare. Their question, though dishonest, brought from Jesus His clearest teaching concerning marriage and divorce.

In dealing with the distressing problem of divorce, Jesus sought to get His contemporaries to understand Genesis 1:27; 2:24. "Have ye not read," he said, "that he which made them at the beginning made them male and female?" God instituted marriage as a union. This union was divine; God joined people together in Christian marriage. This union was physical; the two people became one flesh. This union was exclusive; a man and woman were to cleave to one another to the exclusion of everyone else. This union was permanent; what God had joined together, man was not to put asunder. Jesus sought to focus their attention on marriage, not divorce.

In response to Jesus, the Pharisees asked, "Why then did Moses command to give a bill of divorcement, and to put her away?" The reference here is to Deuteronomy 24:1, where Moses allowed divorce. However, the Pharisees held that Moses commanded divorce. Jesus, interpreting their legalistic thought, replied that Moses permitted divorce only because of the hardness of the hearts of the people. Then Jesus referred them once again to God's ideal: "From the beginning it was not so." He continued, "And I say unto you, whosoever shall put away his wife, except it be for fornication and shall marry another committeth adultery; and whoso marrieth her that is put away doth commit adultery" (Matt. 19:9). The Revised Standard Version reads, "except on the ground of unchastity." Weymouth translates it the same way. Dr. A. T. Robertson, the famous Greek scholar, translates it the same way. What Jesus said in these verses is there is only one ground upon which divorce is permitted, and that is sexual unfaithfulness—whether you call it unchastity, adultery, or fornication. In Matthew 5:32, Jesus said essentially the same thing that He did in Matthew 19:9: "But I say unto you, That whosoever shall put away his wife, saving for the cause of fornication, causeth her to commit adultery; and whosoever shall marry her that is divorced committeth adultery."

Some scholars deny this interpretation for Matthew 19:9 because Luke 16:8 omits the exception clause. Moreover, Mark 10:11, parallel account to Matthew 19:9, omits it. Those who deny the above interpretation for Matthew 19:9 say there is no ground for divorce. In answer to these arguments, one should notice that Luke 16:8 represents a different occasion from Matthew's account. And Mark's account records a statement to the disciples after Jesus' answer to the Pharisees. Why, then, was the exception clause used in Matthew 19:9? Jesus was giving a direct answer to the Pharisees' question as recorded in Matthew 19:3, "for every cause."

Permit me to draw three conclusions from these verses of Scripture.

(1) Jesus said that, upon the grounds of unchastity, divorce is permitted or allowed; it is not commanded. Jesus never commanded divorce on any grounds. He said it would be permitted or allowed on the ground of unchastity, fornication, or adultery. There is no evidence in the New Testament that a man who continues to live with his wife who has been adulterous will be guilty of living in adultery. The implication is that it is God's will that they stay together for life if at all possible.

(2) Anyone who puts away his marriage partner for any reason other than adultery and remarries lives in adultery according to the teaching of Jesus. This may not be what we like to hear, but it is exactly what Jesus said. It is virtually impossible to interpret it otherwise.

(3) While it is not specifically stated in the passage, it is implied that the innocent party is free to remarry. The Pharisees asked, "Is it lawful for a man to put away his wife for every cause?" And he answered, "Whosoever shall put away his wife except it be for fornication, committeth adultery." Now remember that the Jews to whom Jesus spoke knew nothing of divorce without the privilege of remarriage. They had practiced remarriage since the day of Moses. The only reason they needed a bill of divorcement was in order to get remarried. So Jesus said that the innocent party was free to be remarried.

THE CHRISTIAN PRINCIPLE IN LIFE SITUATIONS

Having discussed the ideal statement of Jesus, let us seek to apply it to life situations. You see, we must deal with people where they are. This is God's method and, it seems to me, it must also be ours. There will always be a tension between the ideal of God and the actions of man with respect to this matter of divorce. This tension should be constructive. It should tend to move us toward God's expectations of us. With this in mind, there are some things I feel we must do in order to be part of the solution to the problem of divorce rather than a part of the problem itself.

In the first place, I believe the church must engage in a positive program of assistance to our people concerning the Christian home. An ounce of prevention is worth a pound of cure! It is our responsibility as Christian parents to see that our children have the opportunity to study in these vital areas. However, I feel that we must go even further. Simply providing an ambulance in the valley is not enough; we must erect a fence at the top of the cliff. We must, in forums and discussions with our youth, engage in premarital counseling. I very definitely believe the church should launch out in a pioneer program of "love education." Notice I said "love education," not sex education. This program should be under the supervision of a Christian doctor and other mature adults. Our young people will never understand God's ideal of purity of living without the Christian context, and they must be brought within the framework of the church to hear it. Too long have we refused to understand a serious problem in our midst. We must do more than condemn when wrong occurs; we must strive to help our young people prepare for Christian marriage.

The second thing I think we should do is to preach and hold high God's standard of marriage and divorce just as we do other teachings of the Bible. The church can never condone divorce or the things which produce it. The divorced man and woman would be remiss to expect this, and the church would be wrong to practice it.

In the third place, as Christians, we must forever reject the Pharisaical approach toward those who are divorced. Ostracizing those who are divorced is most unchristian. Throwing stones at particular sins is unrewarding and self-deceiving. Jesus reminded a group of Pharisees of that when he said, "Let him who is without sin cast the first stone." It is our ministry to create a feeling of fellowship and understanding for anyone who has sinned and is seeking God's forgiveness. We should remember that the church is a rehabilitation center for all of us, not a sorority for sophisticated sinners. The sin of divorce—when forgiven by God—should not rule one out of a position of church service any more than the sin of drunkenness or gossip—when they are forgiven by God. We realize, of course, there are some areas of leadership that the Bible forbids to those who have been divorced. It would seem prudent that pastors and deacons, according to I Timothy 3:10, should be men who have never been divorced.

In the fourth place, we must reevaluate our approach to the subject of remarriage. It is a fact that many people who are divorced do remarry. Through the years this has presented to the church a difficult and embarrassing situation. Basically the ministers of the church have taken one of three stands.

Some ministers refuse to officiate at the marriage of anyone who has ever been divorced. Most of these believe the "exception claus" mentioned in Matthew 19:9 does justify remarriage of the "innocent party." However, because it is sometimes impossible and embarrassing to find out who the "innocent party" is, they simply refuse to marry all divorcees. I think this approach overlooks the need of individuals, is not true to Scripture, and seeks to avoid a difficult decision.

There is a second approach which says there is no ground whatever for remarriage for any divorced person. In the main, this group denies the genuineness of the "exception clause." Personally, I feel this approach is also an injustice to the Bible and to the need of individuals.

There is another way. We can call this the rehabilitative or therapeutic approach. Those of us who minister to people in this complex society encounter this problem almost daily. We cannot, we dare not, overlook the needs of people and the ability of our Lord to meet these needs. Many have come to me for help, therefore, I can say from experience and from the truth of God's Word there is room for forgiveness at the foot of the cross for any sin save one. That is the sin of unbelief, *not the sin of divorce and remarriage.* "If we confess our sins, he is faithful and just to forgive us our sins, and to cleanse us from all unrighteousness" (I John 1:9). We can be assured that God is merciful and forgiving.

To those who are divorced I say, "Make every effort to find the reasons for failure in marriage. Learn from past mistakes and show new maturity which will be invaluable in any future marriage. Seek the counsel of your pastor or other qualified persons in a sincere effort to understand your problem. Relate yourself to Christ, receive His forgiveness, and know and do His will." When I find someone who has failed in marriage, who is vitally interested in a Christian home, who is willing to go through counseling procedures, I will seek to help him.

If one has been involved in a tragic divorce, the answer to a new life and a new marriage lies in the practice of Christian love in the home.

In the Old Testament there is a wonderful story about incredible love. It concerns one of God's servants, Hosea, and his wife, Gomer. Gomer left her home and became a woman of the street. She was anything but what she should be. Hosea went into the streets and slave markets, found his wife, brought her home, and loved her again in spite of the way she had acted. He did this because he really loved her. He loved her the way God loved him—in spite of his wrongs. When we learn to love like that, our marriages will succeed. Therefore, whether we are attempting to prevent or correct "Divorce American Style," the answer is the practice of Christian love.

CHAPTER 6

THE CASE AGAINST GAMBLING

Ralph A. Phelps, Jr.

As Jesus hung on the cross, His executioners rolled dice to see who would get the clothes off His back. Incongruous as the scene was—the Son of God dying for sinners while sinners shot craps for His garments—the soldiers were no more misguided or deluded than are millions of people today. They breathlessly watch the dice roll, anxiously listen to the click of the ball in the roulette wheel, feverishly clutch their ticket while horses' hooves pound the track, eagerly wait while the slot machine whirls, or nervously scan the football results to see who won the office football pool. Human nature, little changed in two thousand years, still hopes that Lady Luck will give a man something for nothing.

Gambling has become such a part of everyday life in America that few people realize what gambling is or give any thought to the peril it represents. As a matter of fact, most of the people who "match" to see who pays for the drinks at the coffee break, who buy a chance on a car for a worthy charity, or who attend a church bazaar where bingo is played or a cake is raffled off do not think of themselves as gamblers. They would not like to be classified with the casino devotees or the participants in all-night poker games. But while there are unquestionably degrees of gambling and gambling addiction, certain elements are common. And the end product is social destruction.

Many are clamoring to legalize and tax gambling since "it is an inevitable facet of human nature," as they put it. Before buying that idea, America needs to take a hard look at the big business of gambling. The late Senator Estes Kefauver, after his thorough investigation of gambling and related criminal activities, declared, "Gambling produces nothing and adds nothing to the economy or society of our nation. America will be in a bad way if we ever have to resort to taxing crime and immorality for the purpose of raising revenue to operate our institutions."[1] Let us see what basis he had for this statement.

Gambling has at least five indictments against it:

THE MORAL INDICTMENT

Gambling is morally wrong; legalizing a vice does not make a virtue of it. Gambling violates at least two fundamental laws of God—the commandment forbidding coveting and the law demanding work. In many cases, the law against stealing is also violated; in fact, the popular name for slot machines, "one-armed bandits," is most appropriate.

Gambling preys on two human weaknesses: the widespread desire to get something for nothing and the frailties of the compulsive gambler, who cannot quit even when down to his last dime. For the Christian, the laws of love and consideration for one's brother are paramount. Trying to beat one's fellow-man out of his money or taking advantage of his weaknesses could not, by any stretch of the imagination, be called the fulfillment of the law of love. Paul went so far as to say, "If meat make my brother to offend, I will eat no flesh while the world standeth, lest I make my brother to offend" (I Cor. 8:13). Although unredeemed people can hardly be expected to follow his high standard, it is the Christian's duty to try to inculcate New Testament principles into society and to follow those principles himself.

Ministers who have occasionally dared lift their voices against gambling have been termed everything from "unprogressive" to blue-nosed spoil-sports for suggesting that a moral principle was involved. Shut out their voices, then, and listen to George Washington, who was not a minister:

This is a vice which is productive of every possible evil, equally injurious to the morals and health of its votaries. It is the

---

[1] Ed Reid and Ovid Demaris, *The Green Felt Jungle* (New York: Pocket Books, Inc., 1964), p. 81.

child of avarice, the brother of iniquity, and the father of mischief. It has been the ruin of many worthy families, the loss of many a man's honor, and the cause of suicide . . . In a word, few gain by this abominable practice, while thousands are injured.

Revealing how timely his statement is, statistics show that the ratio of suicides in Las Vegas, which has pulled out all the stops to legalize gambling, is the highest for any city in the world —30.1 per 100,000 as opposed to the national average of 1.9.

No moral angle involved? Listen to Ed Reid and Ovid Damaris, two journalists who have gone behind the bright lights to tell the shocking story of Las Vegas in *The Green Felt Jungle:*

The city fosters crime as a stone thrown into water creates concentric circles. A tourist who loses his life savings in Las Vegas is just as apt to return home and embezzle, or rob, or burglarize, or steal, or commit suicide (one Reno loser allegedly shot the pilot of an airliner and took 44 others with him to his death), as the criminal resident.[2]

THE ECONOMIC INDICTMENT

Gambling is big business—and bad business. John Scarne, who has made a study of gambling for many years, testified before the McClellan committee that the annual gross figure on illegal gambling involved about fifty billion dollars. Senator McClellan pointed out that if this figure is accurate, the government is being cheated of some five billion dollars a year in taxes. The government as well as the suckers is getting clipped!

No one knows exactly how much money is bet in illegal gambling each year, but four times more money is spent on legal gambling than on higher education. If the total wagered was fifty billion dollars this was some eight billion dollars more than was spent for national defense.

Arthur A. Smith, Ph.D., is vice-president and economist of the billion dollar First National Bank in Dallas and former head of the Department of Economics at Southern Methodist University. He made this statement to the Texas Legislature when it was considering legalized betting:

---

[2]*Ibid.*, p. 180.

Gambling, as defined properly in economics, designates (1) the deliberate creation of risks of a kind not inherent in or necessary to the functioning of economic society and (2) the deliberate wagering or staking of valuable considerations upon events which, so far as the parties to the wager can know, lie in the realm of pure chance, or luck.

It is clear from the definition of gambling that it is an activity which contributes nothing worthwhile in the economic sense. It adds nothing to the sum total of good to be consumed. What one party may gain another must lose, and in the process the winner has contributed nothing to society. He reaps but does not sow. Therefore, gambling is merely a distributive force and cannot be brought by economic analysis within the category of productive forces.

Gambling does not enhance the people's level of living one bit—on the contrary, it tends to lower the level of living, because legalized gambling tends to attract in disproportionate numbers, people in low income brackets.[3]

Chance-taking is a part of many aspects of living. But it is important to remember that risks created in gambling do not have to be created for the benefit of society. A farmer takes a chance when he plants seed in the spring, but there is no other way to make a harvest. Dr. Smith points out that "gambling, on the contrary, involves artificial risks which do not have to exist, nor does anyone have to assume them. They produce nothing.

These artificial risks are further compounded by the fact that the person running the gambling house is not gambling. His profit is assured by the odds favoring the house and by the way the slot machines are rigged so that anyone who plays them long enough will eventually go broke. When a person learns enough about the operation of certain gambling games to have an even chance or better, he is barred from the casinos. Reid and Demaris said of Prof. Thorp, the New Mexico State University mathematics professor who developed an unbeatable system of blackjack:

The professor was victimized by crooked dealers in almost all the major casinos in Nevada. He has been backed off (thrown out) by pit bosses, he has been harassed by shills, plied endlessly

[3]Arthur A. Smith, *Statement in Opposition to Legalized Betting on Horse Racing* (Dallas: By the author, 1961), p. 1.

with booze, eyed significantly by plug-uglies and, on two occasions, rendered spectacularly rubber-legged and goggled-eyed by knock-out drops courtesy of the house.[4]

Little wonder that a standard saying in Las Vegas is, "The surest way to beat Las Vegas is to get off the plane that has taken you there and walk straight into the propeller."

Because gaming enterprises are run on the basis of not giving the sucker an even chance, gambling produces fabulous profits for the operators. Tremendous sums of money, taken from legitimate expenditures for groceries, medical care, rent, or insurance, are put into the pockets of syndicated gambling.

Robert F. Kennedy, who gained insight into the methods of gamblers and syndicated crime while he was chief counsel for the Senate committee investigating racketeers and gambling, said:

Their dimes, quarters, and dollars do not stay in the pockets of the big-time gamblers and racketeers. Just as legitimate business men invest their profits in other businesses, so do the capitalists of crime use their gambling profits to invest in other criminal businesses. High on the list is narcotics.[5]

The authors of *The Green Felt Jungle* wrote:

Some of the money is fed back directly into criminal activities: narcotics, prostitution, corruption of public officials, and when necessary, murder.

The rest of it is invested in legitimate ventures . . . . In this way, the mob has been able to gain control of large private and corporate enterprises where they often apply the muscle tactics that have served them so well in the underworld.[6]

One of the most revealing books written about the path of unsavory gambling millions is *Gambler's Money* by Wallace Turner. He shows how this "black money" finds its way into countless corners of American life and corrupts everything it touches.

Dr. Arthur Smith sums up the economic case when he says

[4]Reid and Demaris, *op. cit.,* p. 207.
[5]Robert F. Kennedy, "The Baleful Influence of Gambling," *The Atlantic Monthly,* April 1962, p. 78.
[6]Reid and Demaris, *op. cit.,* p. 213.

that "there is no economic justification for any kind of legalized gambling—slot machines, roulette, betting on horse racing, or any other kind."[7]

Even the claim that legalized gambling produces tax revenues may be an illusion. Senator Alexander Wiley of Wisconsin, speaking in the Senate, warned the new state of Alaska against thinking that this was a revenue raiser. Every dollar raised from such sources, he said, meant five dollars spent "in higher police costs, higher court costs, higher penitentiary costs, and higher relief costs." And then the senator asked pointedly, "How can one establish greater morality by condoning immorality?"

It is not true that legalized gambling involves only wealthy people who can afford to lose the money. Merchants in towns near race tracks say that purchases and time payments fall off drastically during the racing season. Nevada had to pass a law forbidding pawn shops to loan money on false teeth, eye glasses, and hearing aids! A pit boss at one of the plush Las Vegas joints said, "People in the rest of the world merely go broke and die broke. In Vegas, you live broke."

THE POLITICAL INDICTMENT

All gambling, whether legal or illegal, corrupts; and the more extensive the gambling, the more extensive the corruption. Speaking of Nevada's experience, Fred J. Cook, in a special issue of *The Nation* devoted to gambling, said:

This seems to speak eloquently of a simple truth—that nothing corrupts faster than easy money and that no money is easier, faster, more corruptive than gambling money . . . . It is certainly no coincidence that both Reno and Las Vegas have had to maintain exceptionally large and costly police forces for their size, a marshaling of uniformed power that in itself attests to the difficulty of maintaining order in a gambling society, in an atmosphere of easy virtue where all distinctions become blurred.[8]

---

[7]Smith, *op. cit.*, p. 3.
[8]"Gambling, Inc.—Treasure Chest of the Underworld," *The Nation*, October 22, 1960, pp. 310-316.

It is understandable that gambling should be politically corrupting in the light of the amount of money at stake, for criminals follow the scent of money as a good bird dog follows a covey of quail. If gambling is legalized, the payoff is for getting to keeping a license. If it is illegal, the payoff is for looking the other way while the law is violated. Payoffs for large-scale illegal gambling "privileges" may extend all the way to the governor's office.

U.S. Judge Merrill, weighing the Nevada Tax Commission's suspension of a prominent Las Vegas hotel's license, observed:

Throughout this country gambling has necessarily surrounded itself with an aura of crime and corruption. Those in management of this pursuit who have succeeded have done so not only through a disregard of law, but in a competitive world, through a superior talent for the corruption of those in authority.[9]

Undesirable as illegal gambling is, it may have advantages politically over legalized gaming. In his report to the United States Senate, Senator Kefauver said:

The profits which have been taken from gambling operations are far greater than those which can be earned quickly in any other business. The availability of huge sums of cash and the incentive to control political action result in gamblers and racketeers too often taking part in government.

In states where gambling is illegal, this alliance of gamblers, gangsters, and government will yield to the spot-light of publicity and the pressure of public opinion, but where gambling receives a cloak of respectability through legalization, there is no weapon which can be used to keep the gamblers and their money out of politics.[10]

The political case, like the moral and the economic, is also overwhelmingly against legalized gambling.

THE SOCIAL INDICTMENT

Anything which increases juvenile delinquency and other forms of crime, promotes the narcotic traffic, encourages prostitution, permits invasion of legitimate business by under world in-

---

9Reid and Demaris, *op. cit.*, p. 216.
10*Ibid.*, p. 129.

terests, or bribes intercollegiate athletes to throw contests or fix point spreads is socially indefensible. Gambling has done all of these things, and men and women who place what they consider an innocent two-dollar bet with bookmakers are contributing to these evils. Gambling, tightly controlled by syndicated criminal elements, is the major source of the under world's revenue.

Nevada, which prides itself on being the gambling capital of the western hemisphere, provides a prime example of criminal influences of this "sport." Juvenile delinquency there is more than twice the national average, and the state is outstanding in such dubious honors as murder, robbery, auto theft, and forcible rape.

Embezzlement is a major social problem in this country with an estimated five hundred million dollars a year being stolen in this manner. The United States Fidelity and Guaranty Company of Baltimore made a study of known causes for embezzlement. It found that from 30 to 75 percent of the sums embezzled was attributed to gambling. The newspapers recently told the tragic story of the trusted businessman who had embezzled a large sum of money from his firm and who took his life rather than face charges. But the accounts did not tell that he stole the funds to try to pay professional gamblers to whom he was hopelessly in debt.

It is also a well-documented fact that competition between managers of gambling for a corner on the "sucker" market has led to gangland wars and reprisal murders. Some of these are documented at length and in gory detail in *The Green Felt Jungle*. The televised hearings about the Cosa Nostra also spelled out in detail the tactics of the hoodlum empire. And when an international narcotics ring was recently broken, two of the twenty-four defendants were murdered before they could be convicted.

No list of the social results of legalized casino gambling should leave out prostitution. Reid and Demaris state, "There are two things Las Vegas has in greater ratio than any other city in the world: money and whores." They then point out that in one way or another a conservative 10 percent of its 64,405 population are engaged in the pursuit of prostitution. Their explanation of the chain reaction of a legalized gambling economy is shocking but quite understandable:

Where there's easy money, there are whores; it's that basic. Taken in logical sequence, it goes like this: where there's gambling, there's easy money, where there's easy money there are whores, where there are whores there's extortion and narcotics, and where there's narcotics there's everything else.[11]

We should be reminded again that this is the picture under the "rigid control" of legalized casino gambling.

Men ranging from bank presidents to social workers are decrying the all-too-prevalent attitude of a great number of people who are trying to get something for nothing in today's world. Yet behind the glittering lights and big name entertainers of the casinos the false hope is held that this will be the reward for the player who walks into the casino web: to hit one big jackpot, win one giant pot on the whirl of the wheel, the roll of the dice, or the cut of the card. Hoping to get wealth for nothing except the favorable smile of Dame Fortune is the mainspring that keeps the gambler going and makes the gambling operator rich.

The close relationship of syndicate-controlled gambling and syndicate-controlled narcotics traffic has been spelled out in detail in several congressional hearings. The big money needed to engage in narcotics trade is supplied by gambling, which then increases its earnings even more through the work of pushers.

Gambling earnings have also been invested in businesses ranging from diaper services to meat packing to hotel ownership. The mob brings its muscle along with its money, and the legitimate businessman who is operating honestly finds that his illegitimate competition is impossible to buck. A sizable share of American business is now owned by criminal elements who derived their "stake" from gaming enterprises.

These are the social consequences of gambling: murder, robbery, embezzlement, juvenile delinquency, prostitution, extortion, narcotics traffic, lost businesses, dishonored reputations, and suicides.

THE EDUCATIONAL INDICTMENT

Legalized gambling is often praised as a possible solution to the nation's tax problems and as a palatable way to provide the

---

11*Ibid.*, p. 93.

dollars needed for mushrooming schools enrollments. Rather than being a constructive answer to school needs, gambling may actually be educationally misleading.

Forrest Rozzell, executive secretary of the Arkansas Education Association, said in the *Arkansas Gazette* during the 1964 attempt to legalize casino gambling in Arkansas, "Legalized gambling . . . is neither desirable nor defensible from any standpoint—economic, social, political, or moral . . . . Legalized gambling can create a whole body of corrupted and perverted moral values."

The presence of legalized gambling in a community can give youth the false impression that work is not necessary to get ahead in life; that all one has to do is back the right horse, draw the right card, or pull the right lever on the slots. No bigger lie could be palmed off! A former football coach in a town which prides itself on a hundred-year-history of wide-open gambling says that this philosophy of "something for nothing" so permeated the young people in that place that it was impossible to produce a winning football team. The boys disdained hard work, for they figured that everything would come if they could just figure out a slick angle to exploit.

Gambling promoters have no real concern for anything except their illicit profits, and they will not hesitate to exploit even school children. A menace of which many parents are not aware is the pinball machine. What keeps a good part of these so-called games of skill in business, however, is not the game itself but the illegal cash payoffs to winners. By putting as much as several dollars in the machine before each game, a player can change the odds and his chances of winning a sum of money. He can also lose large sums in a short time. I know of high school young people who have lost as much as a hundred dollars in an afternoon of pinball playing and of college students who have had to drop out of school because they lost such large sums on these machines.

People pocketing gambling profits are reluctant to give them up. A group of parents asked a store owner across the street from an elementary school to remove pinball machines on which children were spending their lunch money. His reply was that he couldn't afford to take them out.

The harm gambling does to schools and students far outweighs any benefits resulting from taxing legalized gambling. By putting more cash into the pockets of the underworld, which invests its earnings in such ventures as the narcotics traffic, gambling may also "pay off" for young people with additional solicitation by dope pushers. It should never be forgotten that the underworld which controls gambling and narcotics is completely immoral, even where children are concerned.

CONCLUSION

The evidence supporting the moral, economic, political, social and educational indictments of gambling, legal or illegal, is overwhelming. However, in light of the public attitude of easy tolerance of wagering and the widespread involvement of millions of people in regular gambling, specific action needs to be taken. The Christian who is concerned about the problem should:

(1) Be scrupulously careful not to engage in any form of gambling, no matter how harmless it may seem. Although the amount of the bet may be small, the principle involved is large. "Set the believers an example," Paul urged young Timothy (I Tim. 4:12, RSV).

(2) Teach, through every possible medium, the evils and dangers of gambling. One reason why this malignancy has spread so rapidly is the deafening silence in classroom and pulpit and press on the subject. "To him that knoweth to do good and doeth it not, to him it is sin" (James 4:17).

(3) Insist on enforcement of antigambling laws on the books. If politicians or law enforcement officers are reluctant to enforce these statutes, give them some backbone or vote them out of office. Christians should not be timid where political action is the only thing which will get the job done in some cases.

(4) Vigorously oppose any extension of legalized gambling, and encourage other Christians to express their convictions on the issue. After heading a state organization opposed to legalizing casino gambling in Arkansas, I can testify that such a stance can bring abuse, ridicule, harassment, and threats of murder from the gambling elements and their friends. I can testify that a great

number of church people will not take a public stand on the question lest their profits suffer. But I can also testify that the Lord will bless such efforts.

(5) Elevate the lordship of Christ. Only when this becomes more important than pleasure, profit, or popularity to the Christian will he have the convictions and the courage necessary to try to cut out this social and spiritual cancer.

CHAPTER 7

ALCOHOL IN A COMPLEX SOCIETY

Ralph G. Turnbull

When the Christian faith permeated the Roman Empire, it made headway in transforming moral and social conditions through transformed people. Many social evils were rampant in the first century, including immorality and drunkenness. There are accounts of debauchery in the records of the period. Paul found that new converts needed help to stand in the midst of the sordid environment from which they came. If Christianity was to be as "salt" and "light" (Matt. 5:13-16), it must affect the social order. The Christian could not escape responsibility for his social relationships.

Our complex order today seems far removed from that first century, but human nature is the same in its greed, lust, and power. We are members of a social order which requires stewardship of life.

Paul wrote that "every one of us shall give account of himself to God" (Rom. 14:12). He was concerned with the social practices of Christians. Should a Christian go the way of the crowd and follow the easy way of life? Or should a Christian dare to be different in matters of conscience and example before others? Our moral responsibility is marked out for us. Because Christ died for all, we should be ready and willing to act in such a way that no one can find any fault with our manner of life. We should not be the cause of weak persons stumbling and falling.

ACCOUNTABLE TO GOD

In our fast-moving world many people use drugs and stimulants to give them a "lift." The pressure and stress are such that

66

they justify this act as a means to an end. Unfortunately, many acquire habits of indulgence which become their moral and physical undoing.

(1) *Let us throw off . . . put on* (Rom. 13:12b, NEB). The injunction is simple and direct. In this section the need for moral victories is emphasized. The long and dark night of sin will end with the dawning of the day of Christ's coming victory. In this knowledge comes the injunction to act: "The works of darkness" are to be thrown off; the attributes of righteousness are to be put on.

Here is the soul's attire in the splendor of ancient armor. The soldier of that day had a breastplate and used a shield with his weapons of warfare (cf. Eph. 6:10-16). Armor is for defense. The weapons are for offense. The one complements the other. The divine armor is "righteousness" (II Cor. 6:7), and it is the armor "of God" (Eph. 6:11). It is spoken of here as the armor "of light" because the enemy is shrouded in darkness. Light is the best protection against the perils of the dark. By throwing off the works of darkness and putting on the armor of light, a Christian is prepared for the test. Then the works of the devil (I Tim. 3:6,7) and the wiles of the devil (Eph. 6:11) are more than overcome in the strength which God imparts.

(2) *Let us behave with decency* (Rom. 13:13, NEB). A Christian is expected to demonstrate the qualities of goodness and purity before others. We must walk becomingly and show the consistency of our profession. Here are listed a few of the items which are detrimental to ongoing Christian progress. The daytime has less, or so it seems, of the evil items. The time of light does not give evil people much opportunity to reveal their true selves. The light brings its own restraint. But when darkness comes, evil deeds burst forth and multiply. "Men loved darkness rather than light, because their deeds were evil" (John 3:19). The record of crime and vice in any metropolitan area usually lists what happens during the darkness.

The list of evil things is striking, and they are still with us. The public sins are found in reveling and drunkenness; the private sins in debauchery and vice; with the twin sins of tension and discord in quarrels and jealousies. It is striking to find these last two linked with the others and obviously equally condemned with the others. The social whirl of America is characterized by these sins.

Uninhibited individuals with their alcoholic indulgence are found everywhere. Some six million people are victims of this alone. Reliable statistics are not always easy to find. According to Yale's *Quarterly Journal of Studies on Alcohol,* there are millions who suffer from the scourge of alcoholic indulgence. The number of women included is about one million. The problem is acute when we find church people, educators, and social reformers now speaking of alcoholism as a sickness and not a sin. Whatever revised attitudes may be found among society, the Bible still sees the sinfulness of this indulgence. It is the way to unlock and unloose other indecencies of life.

(3) *Let Jesus Christ Himself be the armor* (Rom. 13:14, NEBQ. In the three fold injunction to deal with these ills, this is the key. Moral victories do not just happen. One of today's dangers is the willingness to acquiesce in silence to monstrous evils. It is no light thing to attack vested interest and entrenched evil. Many people recognize the wrongs done to people but are not willing to speak out against the source of the wrongdoing. Only a fraction of church people are moved with enough concern *to do so.* Moral victories come only when dedicated people are willing to stand up and be counted. They are ready to face any criticism or sneer, and they are concerned to assist the unfortunate victims of evil. Paul's word offers the secret of victory—to "put on the Lord Jesus Christ." In so doing we make no provision for indulgence. The positive counteracts the negative. The good cancels out the bad. Sobriety overcomes drunkenness.

One of the difficulties today lies in the removal of the shame connected with alcoholic drinking. Hitherto it was shameful for a woman to enter a tavern or to be seen drinking in public. Now this is commonplace. Yet if a woman becomes an alcoholic, her friends and relatives do not wish her designated a "drunkard." To be an "alcoholic" is not so shameful evidently. The status quo of social standards and the acceptance of drink continues increasingly to damn individuals. Homes are blighted, young lives are ruined, and marriages are broken through alcoholism and attendant indulgences.

If only the church would offer Christ as the solvent of these ills! He is the Savior of the body. He is the Lord and Master who can deliver from besetting sin. When He takes control, there is power to win the victory. We are accountable to God.

RESPONSIBLE FOR OTHERS

Paul's teaching relates man to God and man to man. The Christian not only is accountable to God but is responsible for others.

(1) *No obstacle in a brother's way* (Rom. 14:13-15, NEB). How often this counsel comes in the New Testament! At the heart of the Christian life is this reminder to consider our brothers. Any person who comes within the influence of our life is that brother. We are accountable for our actions and the influence we exert upon others. How dreadful if we cause another to stumble and fall through our actions and habits! We are not to live indulgently in dissipation. Here is where we have to discriminate. We know when we shun evil for good, but there are times when we must choose the better and the best. We may have to omit the legitimate. It is not wrong to eat or drink. If another is outraged by what we eat, we are called upon to deny that behavior even though we may not see it as the other person does. Here is where love enters Christian behavior. Roman Christians were tempted to eat meat once sacrificed to idols, and Paul knew how seducing this practice could be. He personally did not eat that kind of meat so that his new converts might not stumble and fall. The weakness of another is the measure of our toleration and forbearance on behalf of others. Liberty must never become license.

(2) *Be led by the kingdom of God* (Rom. 14:16-18, NEB). The chief principle of guidance in difficult questions lies here. After showing that the kingdom of God is not eating and drinking but righteousness, peace, and joy in the Holy Spirit, Paul offered this principle as the best means of making a decision. If any doubt arises about conduct, relate it to the kingdom of God. Paul was sure this procedure would provide the answer in faith. Because God's kingdom is made up not of eating and drinking but of eternal affairs, the way of decision is clear. The Christian life is in-

ternal and spiritual before it is external and material. We are not to live a selfish life, disregarding the rights of others.

Sometimes a legitimate enjoyment may have to be set aside in the best interests of others. Our aim is to assist others in the Christian life and its development. We dare not indulge and thereby deny help to others. Our attitude and actions at this point are determinative. We need not grieve the weaker brother, and we need not hurt God's work in him.

(3) *Have a clear conviction* (Rom. 14:19-21, NEB). Conscience is active in the Christian life. If we are to keep from causing our weaker brother to stumble, we must obey the light we have received. Because we are to be the children of light and wear the armor of light, we must diffuse the light of the knowledge of Christ. We are to follow the things which make for peace and edification. If we are to assist others to advance in the Christian life, we dare not falter in our decisions in moral problems. Any hesitancy here, and we will cause others to waver. Our convictions are based upon our consciences enlightened by the Holy Spirit.

Thus self-denial is called for several times in this section. It is the principle of the cross in action. We learn to say "no." In verse 21 is the eulogy that it is "good" (or "beautiful") not to do anything which causes another to stumble and fall.

The *summing up* of this teaching lies in the fact that a Christian's relationship to others is seen always in the context of love and in the light of the cross (vs. 15). "For whom Christ died" is a reminder of the cost of our redemption and the fact that Christ's death was for all people. When we see others in the light of the cross, we are ready to be moved with compassion and concern to help others. Self-denial does not seem unreasonable then. Saying "no" to self is not out of line. No man lives to himself. We are tied together in the bundle of life.

In the light of this teaching we readily see how Paul had to speak strong and stern words at times. His age demanded it. The perils of society asked for it. Our modern world is no better. All the temptations of the Roman Empire are multiplied now. We live in a speed-accelerated time. We are in danger from sin all the time. We are asked to remember others. All the indulgent sins of the flesh are here mentioned, but alcoholic indulgence is one of the worst. Proverbs 23:29-35 speaks of the terrifying results of yielding to this temptation. Matthew 18:5-14 tells how our Lord spoke the strongest words of condemnation against those who caused any person to stumble and fall.

Eating and drinking speak of all natural appetites which are legitimate in their time and place under God. But let these get out of hand and disaster follows.

CHAPTER 8

THE MEDICAL VERDICT ON SMOKING

Gordon Maddox, M.D.

Tobacco is a herby plant belonging to the potato family. In the early centuries after the discovery of America, the plant was looked upon somewhat as a miracle drug. It was believed to have healing properties for many diseases. As time went on, it became less mysterious and its value as a medicinal agent declined rapidly. *Today it is known to be of no value in any disease known to man. Its only beneficial use is that of an insecticide.*

To relate the entire story of tobacco would require many volumes. Therefore, this discussion will be limited to just a few of the tragic, harmful effects of tobacco on the human body.

CIGARETTES CAUSE CANCER OF THE LUNGS

The most familiar disease, the one most discussed in lay literature, is lung cancer caused by cigarettes. A quarter of a century ago, when I would talk on this subject before a church group or service club, the talk would be followed by discussions, ridicule, and on numerous occasions by insulting remarks. This was especially true when physicians were in the audience. In those days it was estimated that 80 percent of American physicians smoked, and one who smokes finds it very difficult to refrain from defending his addiction. The subject of lung cancer and its relation to cigarette smoking is no longer a controversial question among the thoracic surgeons whom I know personally; and I have many friends among them. The clinical evidence alone would be sufficient to convince me of the relationship between tobacco and lung cancer.

72

In my own private practice here in America I have never encountered a patient with lung cancer who was not a smoker. While working in Africa with Dr. Jack Walker in a tubercular hospital, in all of the thousands of chest films which we read, I did not see a single lung cancer. Those people do not smoke, mainly because they do not have the money with which to buy the tobacco. In addition to the above evidence, lung cancer has increased at a rate which is exactly parallel with the increase in the money spent for cigarettes. During the three years I spent in graduate work at a large medical center years ago, I saw one lung cancer. Today in that same medical center scores of lung cancers are removed each year.

Through the years experimental cancer work, such as painting the ears of rabbits with the tar in cigarette smoke, has demonstrated—almost without exception—that cancer has developed in the area to which the tar was applied. Not only is there much evidence that cigarettes are the primary cause of lung cancer but we now know that there is a very definite relationship between the number of cigarettes smoked and the instance of this disease. If a person smokes one package per day for a period of twenty years, he has a 10 percent chance of developing lung cancer. This percentage increases so rapidly that the "four pack a day smoker" has a 100 percent chance of developing lung cancer.

These questions are often asked: "What happens to the individual who stops smoking? Will he or will he not develop lung cancer?" If the person has smoked for a number of years, he still has the possibility of developing a cancer during the first year or more after he has stopped. But from there on, the likelihood of developing cancer decreases. After a period of two to four years, this person's chance of developing lung cancer is probably no greater than for the individual who does not smoke.

In 1962 the United States Surgeon General, Dr. Luther L. Terry, appointed a committee of ten outstanding scientists to study tobacco and disease and advise him as to whether or not smoking was a serious health hazard. After an intense and exhaustive study, the ten scientists arrived at the conclusion that cigarette smoking was related to lung cancer, that the risk of developing it increased with the duration of smoking, that it increased with the number of cigarettes smoked per day, and that it diminished with the discontinuance of smoking. Incidentally, one of the members of this committee, who had been a very heavy smoker, developed a lung cancer shortly after the conclusion of the report. His case was reported in the *Readers Digest,* in "The Story of an Ex-Smoker."

CIGARETTES CAUSES ADDICTION

Only in very recent years has much been said about the active ingredient in tobacco, nicotine. This chemical is a very toxic poison, a killer which is as rapid in its action as hydrocyanic acid. To demonstrate how fast it works, all one has to do is dip an applicator into a bottle of pure nicotine and pass it in front of a cat's nose. The cat will die instantly.

A number of changes take place in the human body as the result of the absorption of nicotine. For some unknown reason the human body has a profound affinity for this particular narcotic. For instance, when one inhales smoke from a cigarette, the blood stream will absorb from 93 to 95 percent of the nicotine in the smoke. At first the nicotine acts as a stimulant to the brain cells. This stimulation lasts from seventeen to twenty-one minutes. This is followed by a depression calling for more stimulation. This sequence makes the use of nicotine an addiction not unlike that found in other narcotic drugs. The action of nicotine has been defined as a narcotic which stimulates the cgo and gives one the feeling that he is adequate, thus overcoming his unadmitted inadequacy.

The use of cigarettes is more than a habit, something to do with the hands, or a means of sociability. For example, if one who has become addicted to nicotine is given a cigarette from which all of the nicotine has been removed, he will become very nervous and irritable, similar to the morphine addict who has been given an injection of distilled water. A number of experiments have been performed in which medical students have been given injections of nicotine for a period of time. After two or three weeks of such injectioins, unknown to the student he is given distilled water instead of nicotine. Within a few minutes he becomes quite upset and can readily recognize the difference.

After having subjected themselves to such an experiment, the students all stated that they enjoyed the nicotine much more when given by injection than by the process of smoking cigarettes. One professor who was a heavy smoker decided that he would try the experiment for eighty days on himself. At the end of the period he admitted that he hated to go back to the cigarette method of getting his nicotine.

CIGARETTES CAUSE CONSTRICTION OF THE BLOOD VESSELS, WHICH CAUSES SEVERAL DISEASES

Of all the things which happen to the human body as the result of the absorption of nicotine into the bloodstream, the constriction of the blood vessels themselves is perhaps the most pronounced. When the size of the blood vessel is made smaller, naturally the amount of blood going to the tissues is reduced. This is exactly what nicotine does through its action on the sympathetic nervous system. The reduction of the caliber of the blood vessels, thus carrying less oxygen and nourishment to the tissues, causes a degeneration of tissues in the muscles, the skin, the heart, and every part of the body. To demonstrate the degeneration of skin as the result of cigarette smoking, we performed an experiment in which we had two young ladies estimate the ages of the patients as they came into the clinic. Later, the actual age was obtained and compared with the estimated age. In this particular experiment those who had smoked for a period of eight to twelve years appeared six years older than the same age group who had never smoked. If one wishes to look older than he or she really is, he should start smoking early in life.

While this is the only controlled experiment of this nature that I know of, it is hardly necessary to prove this particular point. Anyone with any power of observation has observed the wrinkled face and degenerated skin of heavy smokers—especially women. If you have never made such an observation, please do so; to further identify heavy smokers, notice that they usually have the repulsive cigarette cough.

However, the constriction of blood vessels of the face is minor compared with some of the other portions of the body. The heart muscle is supplied with blood through two small vessels known as the coronary arteries. Due to the wear and tear of life, all blood vessels degenerate to a certain degree, usually beginning at about the age of forty, but in the case of the smoker there is a marked difference. For example, in the age group ranging from forty to fifty, in the nonsmoker the degenerative process is found in less than one percent, whereas in the smoker in this same age group the degenerative process reaches as high as 5¼ percent.

In that decade of life we see sudden death from a heart attack. This so-called heart attack is an obstruction of one of the two arteries supplying the heart with blood. This obstruction, which is a clot within the blood vessel, is known as a coronary occlusion. In forty years of clinical experience in medicine I have seen but one coronary occlusion in a man under fifty years of age who was a nonsmoker. This individual weighed 303 pounds, was very studious, and at no time got any physical exercise. In such a person, one would expect an early development of the calcium deposits on the blood vessel walls. Among smokers the death rate from this particular kind of a heart attack is 70 percent greater than among nonsmokers.

Life expectancy is reduced considerably in the smoker. The American Cancer Society estimates that the one-pack-a-day smoker dies five years earlier than the nonsmoker. The two-pack-a-day smoker will reduce his life expectancy by seven years, and the life expectancy will be further reduced in the three and four-pack-a-day smokers.

CIGARETTES CAUSE BUERGER'S DISEASE

While it is generally accepted that cigarettes are the primary cause of lung cancer and coronary artery disease, there are of course other contributing factors. Air pollution, which adds to the irritation of the lungs, and overweight, together with the lack of physical exercise, which causes more cholesterol to be deposited on the blood vessel walls, also add to the disease rate.

Such is not the case in Buerger's disease. This condition is caused entirely by smoking. One never encounters a case of Buerger's disease in a nonsmoker. The disease starts with an inflammatory reaction in the blood vessels of the toes, progresses very gradually, and finally causes an obstruction of the blood vessels. When these very small vessels can no longer carry a sufficient amount of blood to the tissues to keep them supplied with oxygen and nourishment, gangrene develops. The degenerative process continues up the blood vessel walls and eventually amputation is necessary. Unfortunately, it is usually necessary to amputate well above the knee in order to secure healing.

Through the years during which I have been teaching in a medical center, I have encountered many of these patients with both legs amputated. Yet they were still smoking, though knowing all the time that eventually the hands and arms would become involved. For some unknown reason the individual with Buerger's disease has a compulsion to smoke. It has been my experience to have one patient with one arm and both legs amputated, who still smoked. I pleaded with this person to stop smoking while he still had one arm left, but he admitted that it would be impossible for him to stop.

What about the man who has developed the disease? Can he be cured if he discontinues the use of tobacco? The answer is, "Yes, if he will completely discontinue it and will stay out of rooms where people are smoking." Only a small percentage of these individuals will do that. One clinician, in following fourteen hundred cases of Buerger's disease over a period of years, found less than one hundred of them who would discontinue smoking and save their legs and arms.

CIGARETTE SMOKING CAUSES EMPHYSEMA

Will cigarette smoking ever be outlawed? Yes, it is quite possible. Twenty-five years ago, in talking on the subject of smoking and health, I made the statement that the first legal action taken would be a warning of the health hazard on packages of cigarettes. I made this speech in Austin, Texas, before an audience in which there were a large number of state senators and representatives. Following the meeting I heard much criticism and ridicule of this prediction. However, in less than twenty-five years this prophecy came true. I would say it is quite possible that cigarettes will someday be outlawed—for many reasons but especially because of one disease known as emphysema.

This is a condition of the lungs, inflammatory in nature, which ultimately causes a dilation of the little air compartments of the lung tissue. This stretching of the air compartments prevents the absorption of oxygen into the bloodstream. As a result, the individual literally smothers to death. The death rate from this disease is increasing faster than from any other disease in the United States. It is estimated that there are now more than one million people suffering from this horrible condition.

From the clinical point of view, the incidence of emphysema is so high among cigarette smokers, as compared with nonsmokers, that it leaves no doubt as to the relationship between emphysema and smoking. Not only do we have the clinical evidence with people but the disease has been produced in dogs. These dogs were forced to inhale cigarette smoke twice each day for a period of one year or more. The lung tissue destroyed in these dogs is indistinguishable pathologically (under miscroscopic examination of the cells) from the lung tissue destroyed in human beings by emphysema.

CIGARETTE SMOKING AFFECTS THE ENTIRE PERSON ADVERSELY

Numerous experiments have been performed in an effort to determine the effect of nicotine on the disposition of animals. Rats, given very small doses of nicotine daily, soon became less active, ate less than normal, and experienced a drying of the hair. Rats which had been on nicotine for three months or longer, when mated, conceived far less often than rats not on nicotine. This condition of sterility was due to a catarrhal inflammation of the cells lining the female reproductive organs. Of the nicotinized rats that did conceive and bear young, the young were smaller at birth compared with those from rats which had not been given nicotine. Furthermore, many of the nicotinized mothers would eat or disown their young.

If nicotine has such a profound effect upon experimental rats, it is plausible to believe that it will affect the personalities and bodies of those who use it. In one of our clinical studies of young women it was found that sterility was more than twice as high in smokers than in nonsmokers. Miscarriage was likewise much higher in the patients who were smokers.

Smoking brings tragic results to its devotees: (1) it causes lung cancer, (2) it brings on addiction, (3) it constricts the blood vessels which causes several diseases, (4) it causes Buerger's disease, (5) it causes emphysema, and (6) it affects the entire person in an adverse way. There is only one safe and sensible medical position in regard to smoking: Do not smoke!

The A.M.A. *News* in a story on December 12, 1966, pointed out that 37 percent of all deaths in the United States in 1964 were possibly related to and connected with cigarette smoking. Tobacco-related diseases killed 253 out of 100,000 Americans in 1950, but 394 out of 100,000 in 1964. Again the medical evidence is such that there is only one and sensible medical position in regard to smoking: Do not smoke!

CHAPTER 9

OBESITY — SIN OR SYMPTOM?

Dolph L. Curb, M.D.

Jesus was called a glutton and a winebibber (Luke 7:34). Was He ample and corpulent of figure? Or was it because He relished the pleasures of the table with unseemly zest? Somehow it is hard to visualize Him in that light, isn't it? Don't we picture Him instead as lean and abstinent, thinking the other picture would be not only un-Christlike, but just a bit sinful? I suspect this superficial idea has some hold on the thinking of about two-thirds of our adult population—the two-thirds being those who themselves are not distinctly overweight. The other one-third, who are, would doubtless protest the unfairness of such an idea (that overweight is sinful). They would stoutly insist that their over-weight problem was a burden imposed on them by an unkind fate, which "turns everything they eat to fat."

As a physician who is frequently consulted by these people, I can tell you that most of them shed their defenses in the privacy of the consultation room. They are heavily guilt ridden and ashamed about their "lack of will power." Moreover, conscientious Christians often feel that their obesity is a sort of sin, or at least an evidence of spiritual shortcoming. Of course, this is also true among many others of my Christian patients who have illnesses of other than "organic" origin, that is, psychosomatic illnesses. Somehow they feel that Christians should be "above such weakness"! This constitutes something of a problem for a Christian doctor, who has the task not only of dealing with the physical and psychological problems, but also of helping them to use their

80

spiritual resources for added therapeutic impetus. Otherwise their misdirected guilt feelings are aggravating causes of illness.

Let us look briefly into some of the physical and psychological features of overeating and obesity. First of all, note that I continue to link the two terms—overeating and obesity—together. Of course it is a fact that two people may eat the same amount of food, and one may become very obese, and the other remain thin. Still I must insist that *whatever* the fat one eats represents, *for him,* overeating! This is basic.

In the human as in all animals, there operates in certain brain centers a delicate regulation between the organism's need for food and the appetite that drives him to eat. When he has eaten enough to supply this need, appetite disappears, leaving a sense of satisfaction. In most animals, and in man under simple, primitive conditions where eating has no other function than keeping him alive, this balance maintains an optimum state of nutrition. Even when an abundance of food is available, no more than moderate fattiness develops—enough to fortify the animal against a future period of food scarcity. Extreme obesity is rare in such animals and men; in fact, in the laboratory it is rather difficult to induce a state of "experimental obesity" in animals, though it can be done.

Why are we civilized humans, then, so frequently prone to overeat and become obese? It is apparent that there are factors which can override nature's balancing mechanism, resulting in eating beyond physiological needs.

Our whole culture of civilization has converted the eating of food into social rituals and customs with other purposes besides staying alive or satisfying hunger for food as such. Indeed, everything is done to induce hunger if it is absent, sustain it when it is present, and revive it when it begins to flag. Eating is a basic ingredient of almost every interpersonal contact of our society, and almost every event where two or three are gathered together is built around partaking of food of some sort. These events often bear no relation to the body's nutritional needs. There are aperitifs and appetizers to stimulate the palate and artful devices to make the table appeal to the eye. The desire is to appeal to people and to arouse them in the direction of partaking of food to the full! Food is such an essential part of hospitality that to refuse it, or even to indulge in it with anything less than gusto, is to offend the host./

Furthermore, whereas animals, at least in the wild or natural state, seek and eat food when they become hungry, humans establish a habit of eating at stated times of the day, regardless of whether they are hungry or not. Thus, the hour on the clock becomes a conditioned reflex which takes the place, or even becomes mistaken for, the sensation of hunger and need for food.

When one considers the overwhelming weight of these factors, the wonder is that obesity is not well nigh universal in our affluent country. Need we therefore consider any other factors? I believe we must at least account for the experience of large numbers of obese individuals who are well aware of all the above conditions and deeply concerned about the harmful effects of obesity on health. They are also distressed and ashamed about their disfigurement. They make repeated and determined efforts to "reduce," yet fail time and again. These are the ones who often seek the doctor's help, and, I regret to say, usually they don't succeed much better on his prescribed diet than they did on their own. This is true even when he adds the "appetite control pill" for which they implore him. Why is this?

Here we come to a consideration of the important "emotional" factors. There is no doubt that one of the most common types of psychological "conversion reaction" is the conversion of some thwarted emotional impulse into a hunger for food. This impulse may be discontent with any of one's roles in life—in family, occupation, or community. Also anxiety, fears, worries, and other such tensions may be converted into a hunger for food. The well-known experience of the smoker who quits cigarettes and promptly gains twenty pounds is an example of this conversion of one unsatisfied yearning for a denied object—smoking—into seeking another form of gratification, food.

It seems to me that here we need to distinguish between the figure of emotionally driven overeating, which is an involuntary, and almost unconscious mechanism (or at least a mechanism that drives one against his will) and the common misconception most of us have of an obese overeater as a glutton. We visualize such a person as one of low, animalistic instincts, motivated only by self-gratification. We consider him a person who enjoys being fat and the process of getting that way more than anything else in life! This is a grossly inaccurate idea. In fact, of all the obese people I've known, I don't think I've ever met a true "glutton," though I think I may have met some skinny gluttons! At least if we accept what is said in I Samuel 16:7: "The Lord seeth not as man seeth: for man looketh on the outward appearance, but the Lord looketh on the heart." Many people are gluttons in their desires, though it doesn't show outwardly.

Let us now return to the question raised at the beginning— the spiritual implications of overeating and obesity. Several ideas suggest themselves. One is the immorality of unrestrained eating when the world is full of starving people. This is true. However, I don't think it is fair for us slender people to turn an accusing gaze on our obese friends whenever, for example, the missionary from Nigeria shows us his appalling pictures of emaciated waifs with outstretched, begging hands! What we thin ones deny ourselves in excess calories, we may make up in expensive indulgences of other kinds. The obese have not been found, to my knowledge, less generous in giving than the lean types!

Is obesity a sign of desecration of the "temple of the body"? I need not recount here all the well-known facts about harmful effects of overweight on health; they are dwelt upon in every magazine and paper one picks up. For decades life insurance companies have provided us with hard statistics, showing precisely the increased toll taken by obesity in the incidence of serious diseases such as high blood pressure, apoplexy, coronary heart attacks, and diabetes. Moreover, it is a plain fact that fat people just don't live as long, on the average, as normal or underweight people. Furthermore, fat people do not perform efficiently a great many of the useful functions of normal living and working. There can be no question that obesity is a handicap! Surely, the Christian has a responsibility and duty, with regard to his own body, to observe hygienic and temperate rules for the preservation of health.

To take care of one's health requires discipline, and discipline is one of the achievements a person should acquire better by reason of being Christian. However, discipline does not automatically come when a person becomes a Christian. It is a part of the process of maturing. Maturity, you know, is a curious thing, particularly as it applies to intellectual, emotional, and spiritual growth in people. Maturity is capable of becoming "splintered" or split so that various segments of one's faculties grow or mature at entirely different rates. We may become very mature in one area and yet be very immature in another.

The Christian may be mature in his dedication, commitment, and devotion in Christian service, and yet be very immature in other ways, such as the ability to have insight into conflicts within himself. Such conflicts as those between a sense of duty and ambitions to advance are difficult to detect in one's own personality. Consequently, we Christians are heir to psychosomatic disorders just as we are to physical disease, injury, and suffering. A sign of Christian immaturity is the failure to recognize this fact, forgetting that the Lord never promised us immunity from any of these. However, He did promise extra strength with which to cope with them and strong yokes upon which to bear them.

This implies that the very important area of emotional tensions and stresses, as they bear upon the problem of overeating and obesity, is spiritual as well as psychological. A Christian must recognize the possible causes of overeating and obesity in their true light. These ills may be caused by his dissatisfaction with his place in the scheme of things, or his performances and abilities in that place, or the lack of fulfillment of his various needs. If the Christian can objectively *know* himself, he may be able to bring to bear upon his problem not only an intelligent resolution and readjustment, but also his special strength as a Christian. The Christian's special strength may help him turn his thwarted psychological and physical energies into productive and satisfying channels. If the Christian can do this, he may discover that as a generous by-product he has achieved deliverance from his psychosomatic symptoms, including a previously unmanageable obesity.

CHAPTER 10

THE CHRISTIAN'S RESPONSIBILITY TO GOVERNMENT

Ralph G. Turnbull

In all ages the Christian church has found it difficult to give allegiance to the state. Christians are eager to cooperate with and give obedience to the state, but they find occasions when tensions arise. What was true in the first century is increasingly true in this generation. These tensions are found wherever the gospel is proclaimed and whenever a church is established.

In the first century the local community and the state demanded much from Christians. They, more than other citizens, became the target of persecution when a scapegoat was needed, and their religious ideas and ideals often conflicted with the demands of the state. It was very hard to be a Christian in those days. It was not always a simple matter to live under Caesar's rule. Because of his despotism and tyranny, society was split into divisions by the privileged and wealthy in office on the one hand and millions of slaves without rights on the other. As the gospel brought spiritual liberty, it demanded social freedom eventually. How to acquire freedom in civic and social relations and be a law-abiding Christian at the same time was a problem.

Judges 9:7-15 tells a story in which the trees of the forest sought to find a king to rule over them. From the olive tree to the fig tree, from the fig tree to the vine, and from the vine to the bramble (thorn), the story proceeded until the final choice was made. The parabolic tale had its application to Israel, who lost the best and benevolent rule of God and eventually found the thorny and harsh rule of an earthly king like other nations.

A choice of ruler is important. It might be easier for a

Christian to live under a democracy with a president, under a limited monarchy, but some do not think it would be well under a dictator. Yet Paul and his friends demonstrated that Christianity could be lived under the despotism of a Nero.

THE DUTIES OF THE CHRISTIAN-CITIZEN

In this letter the apostle Paul gave directions to the Christians at the heart of the Roman Empire.

(1) *We are under authority* (Rom. 13:1a). "Let every soul be subject to the higher powers." There is no mistaking the import of these words and this command. In that day the church had to live its life in this restricted atmosphere. No doubt there were some then, as now, who thought only of their citizenship "in heaven" (Phil. 3:20) and had no relationship to anything earthly. Some also would shrug their shoulders at the weaknesses and corruptions of civic life, refusing any responsibility for its correction or improvement. There are always those who think that Christianity should be lived under one kind of government and society, not any other. The first century had its turbulent times because of lawlessness and crime. Christians were often made the scapegoats for punishment. It was not easy to accept the authority of the state. Yet duty demanded this if a Christian was to manifest his faith. Submission was expected (cf. I Peter 2:13-17). Submission to the state then was submission to Nero, the despot and tyrant!

(2) *Government is delegated by God* (Rom. 13:1b-5). "There is no authority but by act of God, and the existing authorities are instituted by him" (NEB). Here then is the promise that a Christian can live under a totalitarian regime. As in the Roman Empire, some today have to live and endure under communistic tyranny. We who live in a democratic society are free from the terrors of evil rule, but we should not imagine that those who live under totalitarianism are thereby traitors to the faith. When we look at any civic office in the city or any higher office in the state or the nation and find someone there we cannot respect, we are not thereby exempt from yielding obedience. We must respect the office, which is God-established, although in our hearts we may

lack respect for the person in that office. We dare not be on the side of the lawless and the law-breaker without cause. If we oppose the authority of the state, we oppose divine authority. The honest citizen has no need to fear the policeman; it is the dishonest man who needs to fear.

In this light the state has certain powers given by God. There is the power to rule and establish laws for the good of the citizenry. The state has the authority to try offenders and punish the law-breaker.

It is a sound maxim of public morality that the state should not be responsible for moral wrong except to repress it and punish the wrongdoers. But this does not mean that the state should take upon itself the punishment of all transgressions of the moral law. There have been ages and places in which it was held to be the duty of the state to punish *sin*. Calvin's Geneva, Knox's Scotland, and Puritan New England have known such occasions. But today the state does not take cognizance of private sin until it becomes a public crime. Thus drunkenness is a sin, but it is not an indictable offense in itself. A man cannot be charged or arrested simply for being drunk. He must be drunk and disorderly, drunk and incapable, drunk and causing an obstruction, drunk while driving an automobile, or in some other way affecting public interests. So fornication is also a sin, but it is not an indictable offense until the person creates disorder in so sinning.

All this raises a question about a Christian in relation to the state if the state requires something which is not in accord with a Christian's conscience. Is there a time when a Christian who is usually law-abiding may resist the government? We believe there is—when the state demands something which is morally wrong or when the state persecutes the Christian church. If the state should fail in its duty, a Christian would be justified in action to rectify abuses and omissions.

Rulers are spoken of here as "servants of God," and the word "minister" is used. Paul had occasion to demand rights of protection (Acts 17:12-17; 19:35-41; 22:25). The Christian, in the light of this section, is required to accept and obey the law, but he is also free to testify against the state if the state should violate divine law.

(3) *Taxes are necessary and should be paid* (Rom. 13:6-7). There are benefits in the community where the civic authorities have undertaken to govern wisely and well. Police protection against law-breakers; fire protection; services of water, light, and power—at least in a modern social structure—not to mention education and health services. Here is the demand for a Christian to pay his share of the expenses. Beyond the community is the province, the state, and the nation. Our American nation is blessed by its services of defense and protection which we enjoy, therefore, it is right that we pay our share of these expenses.

Again, if a citizen who is a Christian in all good conscience sees abuses in government expenditures, he has the privilege of calling attention to these and seeking to correct them by persuasion and vote. History has examples where tyranny and corruption have been overcome by fighting and sacrifice (cf. the American Revolution—no taxation without representation). Again a Christian must decide what his actions will be as a citizen in the light of conscience and knowledge. God alone is Lord of the conscience.

In paying taxes Christians are obeying this injunction of Paul. It is clear and simple in essence. The "tribute" may be personal and include property. The "custom" may have to do with goods coming in or going out in business. The "fear" points to a respect for authority and obedience to the law. The "honor" has to do with the attitudes adopted by Christians in relation to the state's representatives in office. Duties of a citizen are shared by Christians who have respect for the divine office of magistrate and governor.

Government will vary from one country to another and even in local communities. Paul recognized that the state was of divine institution. At the point where corruption and abuse entered, he protested by his life and witness for the truth. We may always distinguish between subjection and submission. A Christian in this world may have to suffer in the tension between loyalty and resistance. The overlords of this world have their day, and the Lord of lords will have His. Peter resisted the state—"we must obey God rather than men" (Acts 5:29)—only when Christ's command was clear.

THE DEMANDS OF THE SOCIAL ORDER

The apostle Peter was one with the apostle Paul in his message about a Christian in relation to the state. Peter had similar experiences of tension and trouble, as has been hinted.

(1) *Tests and trials are inevitable* (I Peter 14:12). Persecution was a common experience for Christians in the first century. No matter where they lived in the Roman Empire there were those who opposed them and their message. Knowing that the Kingdom of God was to come at the second advent of Christ and expecting that event to come soon, the early Christians lived with a great *hope*. The night was passing and the day was at hand. They knew that God changed times and seasons and removed kings (cf. Dan. 2:21). They were sustained, therefore, in this hope even as they suffered. Peter, like Paul, found it necessary to encourage his friends to endure even when they questioned the divine position of a Nero as emperor. A Christian suffers because he stabs the conscience of society by his disciplined life and by his refusal to indulge in the sordid.

(2) *Suffering with Christ inescapable* (I Peter 4:13-14). Here Peter recalled the cross and all its attendant events for Christ and for the apostles. The Christian has no insurance against privations of mind and of body. We live a life of risk and danger. Even as Peter had told his readers that they should not be surprised at suffering, he told them of the reward and glory which were to follow. The future glory was certain; it would more than recompense the Christians for their endurance of suffering. There were also the honor and the heritage associated with Christ in His sufferings.

How can a Christian share in Christ's sufferings? When men reject the Christian, they are repeating the rejection of the cross. In this the church is a link or a continuation of the sufferings of the cross. Paul spoke of "filling up what is lacking of the afflictions of Christ" (Col. 1:24). This emphasis is the same as Peter's word of "partaking." Christ suffered as the Savior to redeem men from sin. We suffer by the power of that cross and in the light of the glory that is coming. To suffer or to be reproached for the name of Christ is commendable.

(3) *Dishonorable or honorable reproach* (I Peter 4:15-16). In contrast to a Christian's sufferings for Christ's sake is the possibility of suffering because of our own misdeeds. Evidently some Christians had been guilty of moral lapses. They had come out of the worst conditions of a heathen society. Perhaps a few had been charged with stealing or even murder. These would follow them to shadow their new life. Peter was eager that the new converts should be clear from the start about the high standards of the Christian life. Clear-cut severance from the old ways was necessary. If they were to be reproached at all, let it be because they were Christians and bore the sacred name. From now on there was a new way of moral rectitude.

To be a meddler in other people's affairs is also the way of wrong doing and judgment. A new convert, in excess of zeal, might unwittingly interfere in other people's business. A "busybody" was a pest and detestable. Peter would have none of that among the members of the church.

In our complex world the Christian will find trouble without seeking it. Running counter to the spirit of the age, we are bound to enrage enemies and puzzle the ignorant. Our standards are set over against the counsel of Mr. Worldly-Wiseman.

The demands of the social order in Peter's day found many Christians puzzled as to how to behave. Should they conform to the indulgent life of the majority, or should they stand out against low morals, Peter counseled, even as Paul had done, that one thing mattered: to relate life to their Lord and Master, who had to endure the cross. In that light there was no difficulty in choosing what a Christian should do. When the Lord had endured the cross, He finally "committed His spirit to God the Father." Therefore, if they suffered, they should do the same. God is "the faithful creator" and, therefore, the God who acknowledges His promises and covenant. Whatever the tests and trials of the Christian church, this is true—God is faithful to stand by in the evil hour.

All suffering, then, has this threefold relationship. A Christian is given a share in Christ's suffering; he suffers as a Christian, and he suffers according to God's will (I Peter 4:13, 16, 19). No wonder Peter made this appeal that his friends should be responsible Christians in a society where there was need to show that freedom in Christ did not lead to license in one's way of life. The society and the state also made their demands. Peter stood with Paul in emphasizing the respect due to the state and to all men.

Man is a social being, and a Christian has social obligations. Since government is a God-given institution, the Christian must respect and honor it unless it denies its true function and demands subjection (despotic) without submission (voluntary). It was our Lord who summed up the tension in His day when He took the coin of Rome and asked: "Whose head does it bear, and whose inscription?" (Luke 20:24-26, NEB). To pay Caesar what is due and to pay God what is due is to resolve the conflict. These are two realms and each has its place. The Christian lives in a social realm but also in the spiritual order. He submits to the one for the manifestation of the other.

CHAPTER 11

THE CHRISTIAN'S ROLE IN POLITICAL AFFAIRS

William M. Dyal, Jr.

Periodically, the campaign's bright glare and candidates' speeches bursting in air give proof through the night that the Democratic and Republican parties are still there. The American political phenomenon is much more than election year excitement, however. There is the long hard pull of government: administrative, legislative, judicial, and informative. Talent, courage, and energy are required of many persons at every level of government to make it work.

The major concerns of government must be justice, freedom, equality, fair representation, and taxation. But also there are the common everyday tasks of negotiation, organization, strategy, voter registration, voter education, and voter participation. Politics at its best is a wedding of principle and practice. It is "we the people," not "they."

Despite such a mixture of challenge and need, many people in American life shun political involvement. Many Christians warn, "Don't mix religion and politics!" The old influence of pietism with its indifference to public affairs still exists. Such an outlook considers politics irrelevant to Christian life. Neutrality is urged. But such neutrality is not really genuine, because a "neutral" is usually, if only indirectly, an ally of the established political and social forces. Other Christians resort to the ancient cliche, "Politics is dirty." Thus rationalizing that involvement in public affairs might be sinful, they ignore their citizenship responsibilities.

There is yet another attitude among Christians which is quite

different from these. The theocratic influence would enforce on
the total populace the religious and moral standards of those in
power. The ensuing inequities and injustices in a pluralistic society can be readily predicted.

Nevertheless, politics and religion inevitably intersect in the
United States at many points. Religion was deeply involved in
the beginnings and early history of this nation. The remarkable
documents which established the nation and its political structure
give evidence of the founding fathers' faith. At the same time,
they refused to set up a theocracy but insisted on constitutional
separation of church and state.

Both the nature of Christian faith and the nature of the
American political system call men to responsible citizenship.
Christian faith involves the believer in a witness to his world of the
love, justice, and redemption of his Lord. The American political
system depends for its strength on the informed and active voice
and vote of the total citizenry. Consequently, we cannot separate
our Christian faith from our political decisions as Christians. To
compartmentalize religion and politics today is the sheerest folly.
It is an invitation to isolationism and irrelevance on the part of religion and to irresponsible and corrupt government on the part of
politics.

There must be government. The Bible recognizes government as a God-given institution to maintain order and to provide
justice. The only alternative to allowing the strongest force to
have total power is to establish authority and arbitration which will
make out of many divergent interests and forces some pattern of
cooperation and control.

Thus, the Bible describes the duty of the Christian citizen
to support the state, even to the payment of taxes. He has a responsibility to pray for the leaders. At the same time, he has the
right to criticize the evils and excesses of government and of politics. The Christian also recognizes his ultimate obligation to obey
God rather than the state when its demands conflict with Christian
conscience.

At this latter point, Christians in every age and in every kind
of political setting have agonized over decisions of loyalty and of
personal action. The Christians under the Roman emperors often

chose death rather than deny their faith. Under Hitler, Martin Niemoeller was imprisoned and Dietrich Bonhoeffer executed because they proclaimed God over the Fuehrer. Baptists in Russia have periodically suffered reprisals and severe restrictions. In the United States, Quakers and other Christian conscientous objectors to war have been humiliated and vilified.

The role of a committed Christian in the political order is never easy, either as voter, candidate for office, or elected official. But the role is not a matter of choice, but of necessity. Dag Hammarskjold rightly affirmed for all Christians, "In our era the road to holiness necessarily passes through the world of action".[1]

The world of action for today's Christian citizen is one of excitement and demand. The area of politics is loaded with issues and crises. The scene of action ranges from the local to the international. Towns and cities cope with urban sprawl, decaying inner cities, slums and ghettoes, poverty, juvenile delinquency, crime, prostitution, alcoholism and narcotics addiction, air and water pollution, and the need for expansion of education and health services. How these crises are met will depend in large measure on citizens' voluntary service groups, town and city councils, elected officials, social workers, planning boards, and voters who inform themselves on the efficacy of the plans of action. Without partisan political involvement, a local church can do much to provide information for its members about community needs. The church can also inspire its members to serve, and train them to be effective citizens. The church can raise questions about community apathy or injustice. Wherever humanity is debased, abused, discriminated against, or unfulfilled, a Christian church has a responsibility to seek justice, to express compassion and love, and to serve.

On the national scene a Christian citizen is faced with the growing restlessness of minority groups and the voiceless and powerless members of American society. He recognizes the many areas of potential conflict in big business, big labor, big government, and a mass society. Mobile man, family break-up, and automation add complexity to the scene. War adds fear. The drain of manpower and resources is frustrating and debilitating.

---

[1]*Markings,* trans. Sjoberg and Auden (New York: Alfred A. Knopf, 1965), p. 122.

Christians have a major role to play in humanizing all such issues which tend to dehumanize man. The prophetic witness and lives of Christians can remind men in all places of power of God's judgment over us all. The exemplary service of Christian men and women of courage, truth, and love must always be a moving force in the nation. These courageous Christians will require the stimulus and support of the whole church, rather than its intolerance or unconcern.

On the international scene a Christian is overwhelmed by the variety and urgency of the problems. The agenda for action cuts across national, racial, and linguistic lines. Hunger, malnutrition, and famine stalk man in India and North Brazil. Illiteracy plagues him in Africa and Haiti. Political tyranny strikes fear in him in Cuba, in Paraguay, and Portugal. War destroys him in the Congo, the Near East, and Vietnam.

Yet, no age has ever known such a worldwide aspiration explosion. New nations have emerged; colonial paternalism has faded. Jules Nyerere of Tanzania, East Africa, calls it the "terrible ascent" from one century to another. President Kennedy assessed that if peaceful revolution were impossible, violent revolution would be inevitable. Both kinds are occurring across the world.

A Christian citizen looks at his world exploding with terror and war, but also with revolution and hope. He may recognize in some of the radical change the revolutionary seeds sown by the Christian gospel with its doctrines of individual worth and soul liberty. Because of God's concern for all His creation in all the nations, a Christian believes the whole world to be *his* concern also. His citizenship is local, but it is also universal. Therefore, he is involved in the character of international relations, in the issues before the United Nations, in the kind and extent of foreign aid, in the thrust of United States foreign policy, and in the way both war and peace are waged. The politics of other nations—friendly or hostile—concern him. The welfare of his fellowman, though thousands of miles away (and perhaps, culturally, light years removed), is of deep interest to him.

Resistance to such a world outlook is a major problem confronting the Christian citizen. Neither ultra-nationalism nor super-globalism is a responsible goal. The idea of the family of nations and their interdependence is important.

Nuclear power colors the current world scene a garish red, signaling danger. The accountability of power is a prime issue. A Christian asks of the various political entities: What is being done to balance that power and ultimately to bring a just peace which can supersede arms and military strength? Norman Cousins in an editorial in *Saturday Review* (Nov. 16, 1965) concludes that "the biggest lesson of all to be learned about contemporary civilization is that nothing anyone is doing today makes sense unless it is connected to the making of a genuine peace."

What possible distinction can there be in the claim of being the last generation of men on earth? The question is urgent: whether our political methods of organizing human affairs will or will not lead to the extinction of the human race. The drift toward total conflict can be subtle, however. For this reason, Christian pacifists have an important place in the nations. While many Christians may feel they must reject pacifism for clear and practical reasons, we need the probing voice of the pacifist to remind us of the subtle but swift current of the "war stream."

Reflecting on Vietnam, Richard Goodwin writes:

If large-scale war ever comes, it will not come in a burst of Strangelove madness or a Fail-safe accident but through a long series of acts and decisions, each seemingly reasonable, that will slowly place the great powers in a situation in which they will find it impossible to back down. It will be no one's fault.

It will be the fault of many leaders, politicians, journalists, men and women in a hundred different occupations in many lands who failed to see clearly, or act wisely, or speak articulately. There will be no act of madness, no single villain on whom to discharge guilt; just the flow of history.[2]

A Christian must be a realist. The struggle for power and spheres of influence is a decisive factor in world revolution. Nations may tend to rationalize their passion for power as a desire to aid weaker nations. Even destructive war is glossed over at

---

[2]*Triumph or Tragedy* (New York: Vintage Books, Random House, 1966), pp. 64, 67.

times with the holy-war slogan, "God's on our side." God is thus falsely represented as an ally for partisan ends and values.

A dangerous trap awaits a Christian who subscribes to a false patriotism which equates the nation with the Kingdom of God. At times I hear church members refer to serious clashes between our nation and another with the refrain, "Don't worry, God's on His throne." And I want to say, "Indeed He is. But don't forget that His throne is not located in Washington nor Paris nor Moscow!" To remind our own nation of this truth may not be popularly received, but it is obviously necessary. Otherwise, evil may be baptized by a nation as right and underwritten by the religious forces. Herbert Butterfield describes the problem:

> The greatest menace to our civilization today is the conflict between giant organized systems of self-righteousness—each system only too delighted to find that the other is wicked—each only too glad that the sins give it the pretext for still deeper hatred and animosity. The effect of the whole situation is barbarizing, since both sides take the wickedness of the other as the pretext for insults, atrocities, and loathing; and each side feels that its own severities are not vicious at all, but simply punitive acts and laudable measures of judgment.[3]

Ultranationalism, tolerated or even sanctioned by religion, tends to give rise to extremism. Nazism thus flourished. Concern for man across racial, ethnic, and national boundaries was sacrificed for the cause of the Aryan state. Principles, laws, and decency were flaunted in the name of the new nationalistic cause.

Courage and wisdom are required by today's Christian citizen who would serve his Lord, and who loves his country. Extremists at either end of the political spectrum feed on the weakness and fear of the general populace. The uninformed fall prey to half truth and distortion of facts. Extremists often victimize true patriots in the name of a pseudo-patriotism that would sacrifice freedom for status-quoism and justice for a police state.

Another contemporary problem a Christian citizen faces is the growing spirit of anarchy in the nation. This anarchy has

---

[3]*Christianity, Diplomacy and War* (New York: Abingdon Press, n.d.), p. 43.

many faces: A draft card burner defies the military system; a citizen refuses to pay his taxes; a governor stands in a schoolroom door defying the law of the land. In some places the very words "federal government" inspire catcalls and boos. Candidates for office run on a "hate the federal government" platform. Suspicion and fear of the federal "monster" are whipped up by forces which can gain from the people's ignorance of the fact that, with all its abuses, the reins of government still rest in the hands of the people. In defiance of the Biblical injunction to pray for our leaders, we are in danger of raising up a generation which has little respect for elected officials.

In such a climate a Christian recognizes the delicate tension which exists between being both critic and friend of government. But there is a balance between the two, and to be a critic does not give license for hate nor distortion of truth. It is the Christian's duty to be committed to good government and ready to make the necessary sacrifices.

Christians have come to this hour with a special calling: to be the ministers of reconciliation, the ambassadors of Christ described in the New Testament. In every community and on the national and world scene, Christians can be the bridges of communication between hostile groups and divergent opinions. Christian candidates and officials must rise above petty loyalties and narrow points of view to lead men to a more creative, just, and fulfilling life.

The results can be highly gratifying, as Foy Valentine points out:

Christian citizens who meet the demands of good citizenship are richly rewarded in the personal satisfaction which they experience for having contributed their Christian leaven to the lump of politics. The good government, which by their good citizenship they help to create, exerts untold influence for good in a multiple of ways. One reward of good citizenship is comparative safety on the highways, in the factories, on airplanes, from criminals, and from the continuing threat of such alien ideologies as communism, militarism, and fascism. Another reward is peace, which must be kept by responsible political leaders who are sensitive to the tragedy, suffering, waste, and ruin which are the bitter fruits of war. Justice for minorities, for the underprivileged, and for the oppressed is another extremely important reward of good citizenship.[4]

Citizenship is not an easy task. The charge, "politics is dirty," is not without foundation. Graft, bribery, and machine politics which attempt to eradicate all opposition have left a sordid record. Still, Daniel Grant, professor at Vanderbilt University, calls the idea that politics is dirty a myth and explains:

We Americans have a double standard of morals—one which condemns in politicians and governmental officials behavior which we take for granted for everyone else. We expect the son of a business executive to be brought into the business and be given a right healthy head start and pushed gently but ever so inevitably upward and onward in his father's business. We expect this, but you let a governmental official do this for his son in his particular division of government and it is good front-page, scandalous news, and we call it nepotism rather than family gratitude . . . Gifts from suppliers to the purchasing agent in business corporations or anywhere else are justified as "good will," but if gifts should go to government purchasing agents it is a major corrupt pay-off . . . The politics of running government is no more dirty than the politics of running a bank or a labor union or a trucking company or a church . . . or a college, and it may actually be a bit cleaner just because of the publicity which it gets.[5]

Because the glare of publicity is so bright, the people know what is occurring. There are multitudes of lines of action open to you. There is the honored privilege of petition, of direct contact with officials by letter or personal interview. There are countless study groups, forums, and discussions of the issues. Editorial and news media cover the waterfront of political outlook. You can read for perspective, from conservative to liberal, rather than just for confirmation of your present opinion. You can refuse to be stampeded by charges and name calling. Copies of the most important pending legislation can be obtained and studied and your opinion registered with the lawmakers. You can work in the political party of your choice. Complete agreement with all

---

[4]*Citizenship for Christians* (Nashville: Broadman Press, 1965), p. 18.
[5]Unpublished address to a Christian Citizenship Seminar; Washington, D.C., March, 1964; Sponsored by Christian Life Commission of the Southern Baptist Convention.

the party's policies may not be possible, but the party system is the working framework of government. There candidates for office are initially chosen and platforms and action decided upon. And, of course, you register and vote.

One of the most difficult problems for the voter is the responsible evaluation of candidates. The incredible American political rites often hide the true person and his true character. Babybussing, beauty contests, bands, train and jet quick stops, greasepaint and floodlights, and phenomenal campaign expenditures are a charade. Often good men refuse to run for office because they are repelled by the theatrical atmosphere. The simplifiers and sloganeers abound in politics. Crowds tend to love homespun emotionalism and oversimplification, which may only cloud the issues or give the impression that the candidate is genuine and a solid citizen. The noted sociologist David Riesman observes with candor:

Forced to choose between skill and sincerity, many of the audience prefer the latter. They are tolerant of bumblers and obvious ineptness if the leader tries hard. . . .
Just because such a premium is put on sincerity, a premium is put on faking it.[5]

A "Christian's eye-view" of a candidate may necessitate evaluating: (1) his stand, public and private, on the key issues; (2) his past performance; (3) his voting record, his endorsements, his campaign promises; and (4) his integrity. In evaluating integrity, church membership is certainly not the only measure, nor even the best. Consistency of character in morality and judgment is important. For example, a candidate may be a protagonist for legislation controlling gambling and liquor interests but at the same time a racist fighting any effort to obtain justice for a minority group. The inconsistency should be noted. Or a candidate may be a family man and church member, but he may lie about the use of campaign funds or accept money from special interest groups who will attempt to control him thereafter.

---

[5] *The Lonely Crowd* (Garden City: Doubleday Anchor Book, 1953), pp. 226-227.

Obviously, no politician is a moral superman. As with all humanity, he has errors and sin. However, his use of religious vocabulary to mask personal immorality or hate or graft is phoniness and political quackery. A chink in a man's moral armor will eventually crack wide enough to show his real character. He is not then to be trusted with representing his fellows in public office.

How important it is for Christian churches to inspire their finest youth to consider politics as an honorable career! Without overlooking the church-related vocations, a church may provide opportunities for young people to meet men and women who serve the community, the nation, and the world at every level of government. Encouragement is needed by the Christians who choose to prepare themselves for a political career. Yet, too often the churches have tried to dissuade them or have rejected them.

Another important frontier the churches and theological seminaries should explore is the urgent need for a politically informed clergy and laity. Christians, who must be the contemporary reconcilers in political conflict, are often inept and uninformed. Key areas of training and information should be programmed from a Christian perspective. What does the gospel require of individual Christians and of churches with regard to public opinion and foreign policy, the needs of emerging nations, moral issues, Christianity and communism, the rights of minorities, the right of dissent, and the legitimate channels for the exercise of power? Christians have a vital role to play in discovering strategies to relieve hostility, injustice, suffering, intimidation, corruption, and fear, all of which are powerful causes of violence.

At the heart of today's citizenship is the painful task of seeking through politics to maintain a proper balance between freedom of the person and the organized action of government for the sake of the public welfare. All government involves constant compromises between the understandable desire of the individual to go his own way and the restraints necessarily imposed on him to share in responsibility to others and in contribution to the general welfare. Reinhold Niebuhr eloquently explores this dilemma: "We can no longer buy the highest satisfactions of the individual life at the expense of social injustice. We cannot build our individual ladders to heaven and leave the total human enterprise unredeemed of its excesses and corruptions."[6]

The strongest and clearest mandate a Christian has for assessment of his role in public affairs are the two basic commandments given by Christ. And he said to him, "You shall love the Lord your God with all your heart, and with all your soul, and with all your mind. This is the great and first commandment. And a second is like it, You shall love your neighbor as yourself. On these two commandments depend all the law and the prophets" (Matt. 22:37-40, RSV). These represent the major thrust of a Christian life and provide him with bases for making political choices and decisions.

He recognizes first that ultimate love, loyalty, and accountability belong to God. He acknowledges God as judge over all human events and systems. For him, God cannot be the special deity of Democrats or Republicans, nor of whites or blacks, nor of Americans or Russians, nor of Southerners or Northeners, nor of rich or poor, nor of advanced or developing nations. This knowledge of God has a levelling and equalizing influence in a Christian's decisions. His love of a just God requires of him justice in his relationships.

A Christian's perspective in politics is also highly influenced by his commitment to respond to God's love for all men, to seek the well-being of others as he would seek his own. He crosses over traditional barriers in this affirmative, out-going concern for the world's "others." Political affiliation and service may of practical necessity bear the party label, but they are not blindly partisan. And they are flexible in application to human need, to morality, and to justice. In response to Christ's commandment, Christian love is the major motivation and measurement of a life. It is no less so in the realm of politics and government.

Again, Niebuhr gives insight into the Christian in politics:

In summary, the Christian faith finds the final clue to the meaning of life and history in the Christ Whose goodness is at once the virtue which man ought, but does not, achieve in history, and

---

[6]*Moral Man and Immoral Society* (New York: Charles Scribner's Sons, 1932), p. 271.

the revelation of a divine mercy which understands and resolves the perpetual contradictions in which history is involved, even on the highest reaches of human achievements. . . . The insistence of the Christian faith that the love of Christ is the final norm of human existence must express itself socially in unwillingness to stop short of the whole human community in expressing our sense of moral responsibility for the life and welfare of others.[7]

You *can* mix religion and politics. And you *must*. You must for the sake of relevancy in religion and justice in politics.

---

[7]*Reinhold Niebuhr on Politics,* ed., Harry Davis and Robert Good (New York: Charles Scribner's Sons, 1960), pp. 341-342.

CHAPTER 12

THIS QUESTION OF CHURCH AND STATE

J. Wallace Hamilton

In the Temple that week there was this quarrel about taxes. There's always a quarrel about taxes. Shall we pay tribute to Caesar? It was a question to trap Jesus. But behind it was another question, a bigger question which hasn't been settled yet. Their big question was how to survive as a religious people under a government alien to their faith. How could they obey and serve their God when at every turn the Romans ruled and overruled in all the practical affairs of life? Who was the Almighty—God or Caesar? They were up against that question, like millions of people in all ages before and since. Where does God stop being God and Caesar take over? Taxes, for example—shall we pay taxes to Caesar? Show me a coin, He said. Whose image is on it? Caesar's. Then give it to him; let him have it. "Render to Caesar the things that belong to him, and render to God the things that belong to God."

It was a good answer and put in such an unforgettable way that the world has been quoting it ever since. As a basic bedrock principle it cannot be improved. But the interpretation of the principle keeps recurring and has to be thought out afresh in every age and society. What is the relationship between church and state? Where does the line run between what belongs to Caesar and what belongs to God? It's a timely question, very much in the minds of our people now. It's a ticklish question because it touches our lives at the place of our deepest commitments: loyalty to country and loyalty to God. It's a difficult question because there are no neat compartments in our lives which we can label and allocate, this for country and that for God. The loyalties cross each other and very often clash.

And we must probe this problem because it is up before us acutely, because it touches our lives deeply, and because if we could get the question in historical perspective, we could get clearer before us what is the Christian answer to the question.

There are four main concepts of the relation of church and state which have been embodied in the process of history during the course of the Christian era.

The first was the church *superseding* the state. It's not difficult to trace that; we had it for a thousand years, the church *above* the state. When the shaky Roman Empire finally collapsed under the shattering blows of the barbarians, there was no law or leadership in Rome. The Christian church moved into the vacuum. The only institution with any moral strength was the church. The famous epigram of Hobbes, that the Roman church was "the ghost of the dead empire sitting crowned and sceptered among the ruins," was not just a clever figure of speech, it was a clear statement of historic fact. The church inherited the crown, the power of Rome. The church became the state.

The pope ruled with the strong hand of the Caesars. He was Pontifex Maximus, the successor of Caesar. Kings were made or unmade by his decree. Wars were fought, many with the active support of the papal legions. The pope had the army; he had the authority. All that was left of the old Holy Roman Empire took refuge in the Holy Roman Church—its pattern of government, its process of law, its power of control. And for at least a thousand years Rome continued to be the center, the capital of the world.

There came a day when the Church of Rome was weakened, by corruption, by many voices within it calling for reformation. It is not good for the church to be a state. It is not good for the church to move out of the realm of persuasion into the realm of coercion. The church was meant to serve the world, not to control it.

There came a day when the Church of Rome was weakened, and in that process a new pattern of church-state relationship gradually emerged, the church *supported* by the state. Again it is easy to see how it happened. In the Reformation the Church, the one Church, became the churches. And long before the Reformation the old system of feudalism had been breaking up and giving way to a powerful new social force, the rise of nationalism. Little units, under lords and nobles, came together in larger units under emperors and kings, with rivalry between them keen. In fact, the Reformation itself was as much a revolt of Germany against Italy as it was a revolt of the people against the Roman Church. Nation-states came into being. The division was secular as well as spiritual and religion became a matter of geography. Every country had its own church; every nation had its own established religion. In England it was Anglican, the Church of England; in Scotland, the Church of Scotland; in Germany, Switzerland, and Scandinavian lands the influence of Luther, Calvin, Zwingli deeply marked the church. But in each instance the church was now supported by the state.

It's a pattern that still prevails. In England the head of the church is the king or the queen. All church property belongs to the crown. The salary of the clergy and the maintenance of its institutions are borne and paid for by the state. The archbishops are political leaders as well as spiritual shepherds. They have their seat, their vote, in the House of Lords, and they receive their appointment from the government.

But now we move to a real dilemma—the church *supplanted* by the state. Dostoevski, that powerful Russian, had no great love for the Roman Church. He criticized it boldly; but living a hundred years ago and seeing the storm clouds of nihilism and atheism blowing up in Russia, he made one of his characters say that the worst fate of the world was not in the past when the church became a state but was yet to come when the state would become a church. What does a Christian do when the state itself becomes God, takes over the conscience of men, the emotional loyalties once reserved for religion alone, and demands of people their first and total allegiance? How does he render to Caesar what belongs to Caesar and to God what belongs to God when the powerful state assumes the role of both?

We don't have to speculate about that any longer. That day has arrived. Within this century we have seen in one country after another the fulfillment of Dostoevski's prediction, the coming of the God-state, the totalitarian state whose sovereignty is supreme, who will have no other gods before it. It was Machiavelli, I suppose, more than any other who gave impetus to the doctrine that the state is above the law, responsible to no authority but its own; and the church, if there be a church, must bend itself around and be subservient to the state. Hitler, you remember, was always haranguing the people about this. "You can't be Germans and Christians at the same time. You must obey the state!"

What does a Christian do when the great Leviathan moves in, takes over, when the powerful state defies Christian morality, moves in on conscience, and asks of its citizens what as Christians they cannot give? That, I say, is no longer an academic question. It's the terrible dilemma of millions of our fellow Christians in our time. Must Christians always obey the laws of the state even when they conflict with divine laws within their conscience? When and where are Christians justified in disobedience? This is no minor question to be answered from the top of the head.

Much is being said today about civil disobedience. Some of the far-right people who have an obsessive dislike for an honored statesman have scathingly denounced a speech he made in which he said that it was often a mark of honor to be in jail. They said he was giving encouragement to civil disobedience. But most of us would stand with him on that. Some of the world's best people have been in jail: Joseph, Daniel, Jeremiah, Paul—all of the apostles at one time or another—John Bunyan, Martin Niemoeller, Mahatma Gandhi, thousands of priests and preachers and nonconformists in Russia, China, Cuba, East Germany. When you remember that 40 percent of our New Testament was written in jail, it comes home to us that civil disobedience often has been a mark of honor. We have it in our history—the Boston Tea Party and Patrick Henry.

Henry Thoreau was jailed once for refusing to pay his taxes. He paid his school tax and highway tax, but for six years he paid no poll tax. The United States was at war with Mexico in what he thought was a dishonorable war. One day Ralph Waldo Emerson was walking by the jail in Concord and was shocked to see his friend Thoreau peering out through the bars at him. "Henry, what are you doing in there?" And the classic answer came back, "What are you doing out there?"

There's a difference between lawlessness and civil disobedience, as Mahatma Gandhi pointed out. And there are times when a citizen is more loyal to his country in jail than out. When a state enacts laws which Christian conscience can't accept, every man must come to terms with his conscience. And part of the reason we can sit in church in freedom is that someone living before us went to jail.

The early Christians had to face this situation. For awhile they followed the admonition of Paul, "Be subject to the higher powers": Obey the laws of the Empire ordained to maintain order. But there came a time when they couldn't do it, when the Roman rulers demanded that they put incense on Caesar's altar, which was virtually an idolatry, putting the state above God—they couldn't do it. They said, "We must obey God rather than men." They paid for their disobedience with their lives.

The church supplanted by the state—this is certainly no solution to the problem. Christians are taught to obey the law. But our country is not God. To make it so is idolatry. Isn't it something when the words of Christ become subversive, and loyalty to country is more important than loyalty to God?

Now we come to a final, a relatively recent, solution: the church *separated* from the state. This solution was a departure from all that went before it. This still holds within it the promise of the most acceptable solution in a pluralistic society where men of different faiths, who spell God with different letters, can live together in mutual respect, At least they can carry out the spirit of the popular song: "You go to your church, and I'll go to mine, but let's walk along together."

This is a good system. Under it all our churches have lived in reasonable freedom and all of our churches have flourished better than under any other. In the wisdom of those men whose experience in the old world had taught them much, and under the guidance, we believe, of a higher Spirit, it was written down: "Congress shall make no law respecting an establishment of religion or prohibiting the free exercise thereof." Many people wish the writers had enlarged on that, that they had not been so economical with words, that they had gone further in the expression of their intent. But at least this much is clear. Here in this new world there can be no officially recognized state church such as our forefathers knew in Europe, no established church, no church favored above others, no financial support by the state for any church. "It's a tyranny," said Jefferson, "to compel a man to pay a tax to support another man's religion."

This is the clear intent of the First Amendment, to keep the churches free from the control of any state and to keep the state free from the control of any church. It's a good law. That's why some of us are disturbed today by efforts to break it down, why we are vigorously opposed to federal aid to private schools, parochial schools, or church-related schools. What makes them private is their independence. If the government pays the bills, they've lost it. It has never been better stated than by a German Roman Catholic, a Jesuit, Karl Rahner. "The time has come for all Christian churches to give up once and for all the attitude once held by some that they ought to try to become powerful enough to dominate any state, society, or culture. The purpose of the church is to serve the world, not to try to rule it." That makes good sense, and we must hold to this First Amendment, which clearly means we want no church superseding the state or supported by the state or supplanted by the state. We want the church as an institution separated from the state.

Right here comes another problem—a widespread confusion as to just what we're trying to separate: Is it the church from state, or is it religion from life? There's a difference. Millions of people are unhappy now about the Supreme Court decisions with respect to religion in the schools and the far-reaching ramifications of what that decision implies and where it may ultimately lead. What are we trying to separate? Are we, whose roots run deep into religious faith, whose democracy was shaped in large measure by it, to be cut off from it and become a completely secularized state in which even the name of God is legally excluded? Or is this a premature judgment, a misapplication of a principle, the first steps in a radical departure from the intent of the amendment? Where are we going? What do we mean?

Are our children and their children to be taught, at least by in-
ference, that God is not important, not even one fact among all
the facts? Are we prepared to put the whole educational process
on the side of antireligion as in Russia? Is it a constitutional re-
quirement that we make the state irreligious?

These are big questions; they can't be shrugged off, can't be
left to social scientists and constitutional lawyers. They are basic
questions that affect the lives of all of us, and they affect the
lives of our children more than others. How confusing it must be
to children on Sunday to be taught that God is all-important and
on Monday and in the affairs of state that He is of no importance
at all.

Some youngster wrote a little verse about that:

> Now I sit me down in school where praying is against
> the rule,
> For this great nation under God finds public mention
> of him odd;
> Any prayer a class recites now violates the Bill of
> Rights,
> And any time my head I bow—becomes a federal mat-
> ter now.

There's an open end to this question of church and state.
It's a bit of unfinished business that someday must find a better
answer. We can't leave it to the lawyers; it's a task for all of us.

Dean Inge said that dualism of church and state must someday come to an end, and the truths which underlie Hebrew-
Christian religion and Greek philosophy and Roman law can be
brought together in some form of politics which will make room
for both a spiritual commonwealth and a purified patriotism.
Hebrew-Christian religion, Greek philosophy, Roman law, the
very best in the past, brought together in a higher synthesis—
that's one form of polygamy I would like to participate in.

Many times we have sung "America the Beautiful" without
knowing how it was put together. The words are a poem by
Katharine Lee Bates; the music is from an old folk song not
well known. But a Baptist preacher of Rochester brought the

words and music together in a hymn sheet, and it was the late Charles Clayton Morrison who first published it in a hymnal and brought it out into public use. They did something that leaves us deeply in their debt, brought two good things together in a larger beauty. Do you suppose we could do that too, bring the words of our law books and textbooks and the music of our faith into a larger synthesis so that this nation under God may sound a high and holy note among the discordant voices of mankind?

CHAPTER 13

THE CHURCH IN YOUR HOUSE

Gordon Clinard

There are four references in the New Testament to "the church in thy house." Two of these references are to the house of Aquila and Priscilla—those two wonderful Christians who opened their doubtless spacious house to Paul. They extended to him, as they had done to others, matchless friendship, fellowship, and love. Another of the references is to Nymphas, a wonderful Christian at Colossae. And the other reference is to the house of Philemon, to whom Paul wrote asking that this generous and compassionate Christian receive Onesimus, the runaway but now converted slave, back into his house as a brother.

I am sure that the significance of these references is apparent. It was at least the third century before church buildings existed. The church often met in homes for many reasons: Their numbers were small. Their economic resources were meager. They lived in hostile communities where they were oppressed. So they met in homes where the family circle and the servants of the household joined together for worship. Or sometimes, as doubtless in the case of Aquila and Priscilla, the larger house of a more affluent Christian would be opened for worship.

Many lessons flow out of this first-century meeting place for the church. This can teach us that the church is first spiritual before it is institutional. Of course one of our problems is that we always think in terms of the church as institutional. To some of us the building is the church—you come to the building to do church work. Certainly I believe in the institutional church and I believe that we should provide the best buildings possible, adequate for education and worship. But let us remind ourselves that the church is not first an institution. It is the people of God. If some natural calamity or some act of war or dictatorship should keep us from assembling in our building next Sunday, where would the church be? It would be wherever we were, and it could possibly be more virile than it is today!

This New Testament pattern should teach us that it is the church in the world that counts. Now the church must gather—and gather it did in homes—but the church does its mission in the world. It is the Christian who does all of his work for God within the walls of this building or on Sunday who does not understand the mission which is the church. A "church" religion is never enough. Unless it dominates life totally, it is not mature, genuine Christianity.

One could look at this phrase, "the church in thy house," as an eloquent reminder of the primacy of the home. In these days when almost everything seems to occupy our first attention more than the home, it is good to remember that in God's economy the home and family are the primary and most sacred institutions of society. The first nursery was a home. The first school was a home. The first hospital and the first manufacturing plant was a home. And the first church was a home. How different it is now—when education is turned over to the schools, when social life is turned over to civic institutions, when religion is turned over to the institutional church, when welfare is the concern of government. It is good to remember that God has made the home the depository of faith and the trustee of divine grace.

"The church in thy house"—the meaning is obvious, yes, and the lessons for the church and for the home which flow from this ancient meeting place of the people of God are rather obvious. But I seek to lay hold on some meaning not so obvious, and yet true, to be found in the term, "church in thy house." What kind of home would it be for the church to meet in it? What kind of parent would it be who would make his home a place of worship and who would open his house for the assembly of Christians? Calvin saw in this language, "the church in your house," a home in which a father and mother regulate their family relations in the image of the church and where members of a family

live like pastors in their homes. Christian homes should be like
little churches, where the characteristics of the church in its deepest spiritual sense become the dynamics of the family and of the
home. Perhaps this concept can mean something to our homes
in this unique time in which we live.

The church in your house—what does it mean for our families?

THE CHURCH IN THE HOUSE MEANS THAT LOVE IS THE DYNAMIC OF THE HOME

There can be no question that the unity of the church and
the entire dynamic of the church in relationship is love. The
whole emphasis of the New Testament is on the oneness, the
sharing, the fellowship of love in the church. Those early Christians were called "the love community." One of the things which
startled all the ancient world was the way they loved one another.
The whole Christian ethic is an ethic of love. It is a new concern for persons. It is a new relation to God. Persons are to be
loved. Things are to be used. The basest of sins come when we
get them reversed.

So if the church is truly in your house, love is the dynamic
of the family. Some of the meanings of this are obvious. Mature love is the only basis for marriage. It is everywhere in the
Bible—the great love stories of literature reach their apex in the
accounts of the Old Testament lovers. Paul climaxed it all in the
Ephesian passage: "Husbands, love your wives, even as Christ
also loved the church, and gave himself for it." Men ought to
love their wives as their own bodies. The love which alone makes
for successful marriage is mature love. It is the kind of love which
ought to be the heartbeat of the church.

There are various stages of love. There is infant love. What
is the first love of an infant? You may answer: He first loves
his mother. But you are wrong. He first loves himself. Before
long he learns when and how to cry to get everything he wants.
Some of us have never outgrown that love. It will never do as a
basis for marriage. And so it goes—neither will gang love, or
lust confused with love—only mature love. This is like the re-

deemed love of the people of God, as people who think not of themselves but of others, as people who give, as people who desire the best for others.

In the family of God, further, every person is of unique worth. The effectiveness of the whole is realized only in the identity of each. So proper love in the home seeks the right for every person to become a true individual. *Life* Magazine published a series of articles on the struggles of persons in our time to be individuals—they want to know their own identity; they want to be persons, to be accepted for their own worth. It is interesting that in the May 12, 1967, issue the modern family is seen as both helping and hindering the development of individuality. Helping, because the family is no longer the closely knit unit it was; the son no longer feels compelled to follow the profession of his father. Hindering, because the loss of all sense of tradition and authority in the family has led to the strains and conflicts of a young generation in rebellion.

But when love like the love of a church dominates a home, the greatest desire we have is to let each member of the family become a person in the fullest sense. Far too many mothers and fathers impose their own wishes upon their children to the extent that they have no identity left to be persons. The elders are perfectionists, expecting their children to be perfect. Love, on the other hand, will accept people for what they are and seek to bring about their fulfillment. Have you ever seen a parent love an afflicted child? Love knows no difference. The real home loves us for what we are.

If the church is in your house, then the family knows how to heal its hurts. Real love knows how to forgive. What is the fellowship of the church without the willingness to forgive, to bring healing to the hurts of life, to restore one another? So, as Calvin suggested, if the church is in the home, there is a pastor there—someone to lean upon, someone to guide, someone ready to heal the hurts, to forgive the weaknesses and the failures. The spirit of a true Christian home is the spirit of love which looks for restoration of its members.

Certainly, if the church is in your house, there is love.

The Church in the House Means Discipline

The purpose of the church, for one thing, is to prepare people for their mission in the world. This is why we assemble for worship and study. So it is the mission of the Christian home to prepare its members for life. We can well term this the mission of discipline.

We are all concerned about the declining regard for discipline and the fading respect for authority which seem to characterize family life today. The impression you get from contemporary fiction is that youth today are disturbed and disturbing. J. D. Salinger's Holden Caulfield gets into one mess after another. Wright Morris' Jubal Gainer whirls away on his stolen motorcycle from crime to crime. The college student in John Nichols' *The Sterile Cuckoo* major on alcohol and sex. John Hensley in *Too Far to Walk* presents the newest lost generation complete with LSD. Hoodlums in the lower depths appear in *Last Exit to Brooklyn.*

We all know the satire of Al Capp, the originator of Li'l Abner. He was recently asked to give his analysis of modern youth. This is a part of his answer: "When I was six years old, my parents put me in a clean shirt, pointed out the direction of the school, and told me not to come back for eight years. In those years we didn't worry about emotional stability. All children were emotionally unstable. They were full of hatreds and frustrations. Wouldn't you be if you were half the size of the rest of the world and didn't have a nickel to your name? Sure we were unloved—nobody paid any attention to us, and in turn we didn't pick up our father's shotgun and wipe out the whole family. It is my opinion that we should give American children something they need and desperately crave—brutality. We must make them feel neglected, insecure, unwanted, and unloved. In return, we'll get courtesy, obedience, good scholastic records, and fewer parents will be killed. And one thing more—don't be a pal to your son. Be his father. What child needs a forty-year-old man for a friend?"

Has the satirist said anything worth hearing? I suspect that he has. Where there is no authority and discipline in the home, the child can never come to be the person he needs to be. Where there is love, there is discipline. It is true with the family of God; it is true with the home. In the home the child is to be turned in the way he should go.

But let us never think that discipline is basically punitive and negative. Discipline is basically a matter of teaching, of maturing positively. Just as God planned this sort of discipline for the church, so He planned it for the home. The ancient Jewish home felt the burden of religious instruction. The law of God was worn as a sign upon their hands and as frontlets on their foreheads. It was to be spoken in the house and written upon the door posts of the house. In house and temple and synagogue the obligation was to teach. So it is with us today if the church is in our houses. Just as it is the commission of the Christian church to teach all nations, this is the mission of the home—to teach, to mature persons for their role in the world as Christians.

The greatest teaching force is the lesson from life. In the home children learn most by what they see in us. The first impression about marriage comes in the home. The first impression about the church and about God comes in the home. The first impressions about the church and about God comes in the home. The first impressions about honesty and morality come in the home. What our children see and hear in the home will determine life for them tomorrow. The point is, you don't kid the kids. The first step in getting those in the home to go in the right way is to go that way ourselves. It would appear that we are reaping the results of failure in this area.

THE CHURCH IN THE HOUSE MEANS THAT
CHRIST IS LORD OF LIFE

The church is the family of God, the redeemed community. It is God's people, committed in a personal experience to Christ. This community is under the lordship of Jesus. Its only option is to follow Christ and to deliver his word to a distraught world.

If homes are little churches, then Christ must be Lord there. It is in commitment to Christ that marriage, parenthood, and the family come to their highest meanings. In Greek the word for home signified a shrine for the gods. In the Christian meaning of the term that is exactly what the home should be—a place where everyone loves, honors, and follows Christ. When by God's grace a home becomes a citadel of faith, love, and worship, that home becomes a churchlike institution; it is the very vestibule of heaven.

I think it is no accident that the Kingdom of God—even heaven itself—was spoken of in terms of the family. "In my father's house are many rooms" (John 14:1, RSV). "Behold I stand at the door and knock" (Rev. 3:20). "Surely goodness and mercy shall follow me all of the days of my life; and I shall dwell in the house of the Lord forever" (Psalm 23:6, RSV).

A writer tells of taking a high school girl to her home. It was a little house, little more than a shack, really. When she noticed that he looked at the house with some degree of pity, she said, "I know it is not much to look at, but it is a wonderful place to look from."

When that is true, there is a church in your house.

CHAPTER 14

MORAL CRISIS, U.S.A.

William M. Pinson, Jr.

The title "Moral Crisis, U.S.A." may be misleading. It is not intended to imply that the United States has suddenly changed from a land of saints into a land of sinners or that American morals are totally bankrupt. To speak of a former golden age of purity in American life is to demonstrate ignorance of the past. While a dark picture indeed can be painted of present American morals, the canvas—if the artist paints honestly—will not be all dark. Often news-hungry reporters and profit-mad publishers exaggerate and exploit current conditions. In many ways American morality is no worse today than in years past, and in other ways it is better.

The graph of American morality is not one huge downward plunge. There have been gains as well as losses. Certain areas of morality, however, are cause for alarm in contemporary America. In this sense there is a moral crisis. Journalists, scholars, churchmen, politicians, educators, law enforcement officers, and purists have all taken note of the crisis.

Numerous publications—popular, religious, and scholarly— have tumbled from the presses carrying accounts of moral breakdown. One magazine stated, "We are witnessing the death of the old morality."[1] Elton Trueblood, philosopher and religious author, gained recognition because of his analysis of the moral depression. Pitirim Sorokin, eminent Harvard sociologist, termed ours a "sensate culture," and the phrase has been widely repeated.

---

[1]J. Robert Moskin, "Morality USA," *Look,* September 24, 1963, p. 74.

119

Foy Valentine, executive secretary of the Southern Baptist Christian Life Commission, wrote, "Many factors have combined in the present age . . . to produce a state of moral disintegration which may not be new but which is certainly manifested on an unprecedented scale."[2]

J. Lester Harnish, president, American Baptist Convention, has written: America is in a state of crisis. This is not because the paperbacks and the commentators say so, but because the red-necked racists, the wild kids on the beaches, the punks, the beatniks, the pregnant high school girls, the dope addicts, the vandals, the TV addicts, the sick readers of sick books, the sick viewers of sick movies, are saying so.[3]

These dreary evaluations of America's moral state of affairs are not without basis in fact. Signs of decay are distressingly evident.

EVIDENCE OF MORAL CRISIS

Stark naked hate is abroad in the land. A church member stood up to challenge a preacher's sermon on love by shouting, "God is hate!" In November 1963, a crowd in a large city cheered when it was announced that the alleged assassin of President Kennedy had been murdered. During the 1960's, Americans assassinated a president and a senator, spat upon a senator, shouted their desire that an American ambassador to the United Nations burn in hell and the Chief Justice of the Supreme Court of the United States be lynched. In the midst of the racial revolution a group of women gathered outside the home of a Methodist minister who had helped a little Negro girl enter a previously segregated school. Over and over again they chanted, "Nigger lover, nigger lover, nigger lover, Jew! We hate niggers and we hate you!" Too often Americans are guilty of loathing their neighbors rather than loving them.

America is increasingly a nation of criminals. The rise in

---

[2]Foy Valentine, "Christianity and Morality," *The Baptist Messenger,* October 15, 1964, p. 3.

[3]"The Church's Towering Task," *Christianity Today,* January 15, 1965, p. 23.

crime is spectacular. Since 1960 crime has increased over five times faster than the population; crime is up 46 percent, while the population is up only 8 percent! A serious crime takes place every fifteen seconds in the United States. Syndicated crime, such as the Mafia and the Cosa Nostra, increases in influence and power annually.

Juvenile crime also has increased. During the decade 1953-1962, arrests of persons under the age of eighteen climbed 115 percent, while the total number of young people in the ten-seventeen-year age group rose only 47.6 percent. Juveniles currently represent almost 50 percent of the total arrests. These figures do not tell the entire story because a large but undetermined numbr of young people are handled in unofficial proceedings.

Closely related to crime is the dishonesty which is found in all strata of American life. Ignoring speed laws, fixing traffic tickets, padding expense accounts, bribing government officials, cheating on exams, copying term papers, fudging on income tax returns, misrepresenting products in advertisements, and stealing from employers, stores, and businesses have become a part of the American way of life. Apparently nothing is safe from American thievery.

Gambling—which may be defined as stealing by mutual consent—gnaws America's moral fabric. Wealth without work appears to be becoming the national ideal and gambling the national pastime. An estimated fifty million Americans wager fifty billion dollars annually. Gamblers Anonymous, an organization created to help persons addicted to gambling, estimates that four to six million persons in America are compulsive gamblers.

The consumption of alcoholic beverage has also been increasing. In 1952, Americans paid approximately $9,715,000 for 2,926,000 gallons of alcoholic beverage, as compared to $12,134,000 for 3,239,000 gallons in 1962. Since 1946, the percentage of drinkers among adults has risen from 65 to 71. Of those who drink, one in fifteen becomes an alcoholic. Already approximately five million Americans are alcoholics.

Family life in America is increasingly plagued by disruption. The rate of divorce in the United States is the highest in the West. It is three times higher than that of England or West Germany.

Divorce in America is much more prevalent now than in the past century. For example, in 1890 there were 55.6 divorces per 1,000 marriages; in 1959 there were 259 divorces per 1,000 marriages. The number of divorces per 1,000 existing marriages increased from 1.2 in 1860 to 9.3 in 1956. The increasing number of teenage marriages has contributed to family instability. The teenage divorce rate is three times higher than that of the twenty-one to twenty-five year age group.

The most publicized aspect of morals in America is sex. The culture has become sex-saturated. Appeals to sex ooze from billboards, newspapers, magazines, television sets, movie screens, fashion shows, and store windows. Bunny clubs, homosexuals, nudity, call girls, wife trading, and pornography are a prominent part of the American scene.

An increasing number of books and magazines ridicule marriage, encourage sexual promiscuity, laugh at purity, scoff at monogamy. They set forth sexual satisfaction as the *summum bonum* of life, accentuate nudity, and picture women as so much meat to be consumed by men. The volume of pornographic and obscene materials distributed in America has skyrocketed within the past two decades.

Premarital and extramarital sexual relations are common in the United States. On the basis of surveys, Kinsey estimated that 67 percent of college men and 60 percent of college women had sexual intercourse prior to marriage. He also concluded that about 50 percent of all married males and 26 percent of all married females have intercourse with someone other than their mate while they are married.

A number of factors other than surveys indicate the extensiveness of sexual intercourse outside of marriage. Births out of wedlock are increasing. In 1940, 3.8 percent of the live births were of this nature. By 1961, the figure was 5.6 percent. The 89,500 known births out of wedlock in 1940 had increased to 240,200 in 1961. Of these babies, 41 percent were born to teenage mothers.

Of course, out-of-wedlock births do not tell the whole story about sexual practices outside of marriage. Birth control techniques are widely known and frequently practiced. If pregnancy occurs, many girls marry. Surveys indicate that 40-80 percent of the brides under eighteen years of age are pregnant when they marry. Others go the route of abortion. While no official statistics exist, an estimated one million abortions are performed each year in the United States. One devastating effect of sexual looseness has been the increase in venereal disease, especially among young people. From 1956 to 1965, syphilis increased 126 percent among those fifteen to nineteen years old, 185 percent among those twenty to twenty-four, and 270 percent among those twenty-five to twenty-nine. And the increase continues.

The list of areas where moral shoddiness is evident could be continued—race, international relations, politics, labor, business, and others. But the fact of corruption in morality is already well established—in the public as well as private sections of American life.

Factors Contributing to Moral Crisis

When we seek a reason for the widespread moral breakdown and for the changing pattern of ethical standards, we discover a bewildering array of answers. Some answers are inadequate oversimplifications. The common response, "Sin is the cause," while basically true, says too little because it says too much.

Likely, there is no one cause of the crisis. There are, however, many contributing factors. Most of these factors are further evidence of the crisis. In addition, they demonstrate that the crisis encompasses not only actions but attitudes.

Widespread irresponsibility is certainly one contributing factor. A growing number of people have little sense of responsibility for society or for their own actions within society. Irresponsibility can be attributed to several trends in our culture.

For one thing, ours is increasingly a collective society. Bureaucracy dominates government, business, religion, labor, and education. Almost everyone has someone above or below him in a chain of command—someone to whom he can pass the buck, someone he can blame for his own failures. Decisions are largely group decisions, not individual choices. All these factors dull an individual's sense of personal responsibility.

The rootlessness of our way of life has also contributed to irresponsible action. America has become a nation of nomads. Constantly on the move, few have the opportunity or the desire to put roots down and feel a sense of real community responsibility.

Urbanization has tended to sap man's sense of personal responsibility. Once a rural nation, we have become a country of cities. In the cities people rapidly lose their identity as persons, becoming anonymous numbers. It is not that people from small towns and the country are more moral than their city cousins. They simply have fewer opportunities for serious breaches of generally accepted moral codes and feel more restraint from their social environment.

The growing complexity of society has created a sense of helplessness in the individual. A common attitude is, "With life so complex, with problems so large, what good can I as one person do?"

The emphasis on, and wide acceptance of, behavioristic psychology and religious determinism have stimulated an irresponsible attitude in regard to morality. Behavioristic psychology turns man into a fleshly IBM machine into which data is fed and response is made without real freedom. Without freedom there is no responsibility. Behavioristic psychology has provided a rationalization for antisocial acts. Religious determinism, which declares that man is nothing and God is everything, turns men into a robot with no real freedom. Such an attitude does not promote the discipline out of which strong character is created.

Discipline in general is missing from the American moral scene. Affluence, permissiveness, and fun morality have robbed people of the discipline necessary for the development of strong moral muscles.

Closely related to widespread irresponsibility is the general lack of moral urgency in America. Most Americans care little about moral issues. Toleration and moderation have been so much stressed as virtues that moral urgency has fallen into disrepute. The national ideal is to be tolerant of others—their religious beliefs, their moral convictions, their weaknesses. A little cheating, a little graft, a little premarital sex, are considered normal and acceptable. It takes a heinous crime indeed to shock most people.

Despair has also reduced a sense of moral urgency. Some persons despair the continuation of civilization. Convinced that man soon will either bore or burn himself to death, they see no reason for attempting to make a better world. Many despair of making the world better. Convinced that evil is in total control, that the tide of immorality cannot be turned back, they refuse to become involved in efforts to upgrade the moral level of society. Others despair of finding any real meaning in life, of discovering a cause or truth or principle to which they can commit themselves. These pathetic persons consider idealism naive, morality cowardly, and patriotism corny. Shorn of both restraint and hope, they contribute to moral decay.

Boredom also has played a part. Work occupies less and less of the average American's time. Unemployment, shorter hours, and early retirement place in the hands of Americans millions of hours that once were consumed by work. Being work-oriented, most do not know how to use their new-found leisure. Some use it destructively—drinking, gambling, playing with sex. All too often, the blight of boredom is broken by a synthetic excitement of racing autos, risque entertainment, and wanton violence.

The decay of American home life has certainly contributed to moral crisis. Because of cultural influence and personal choice, numerous families neither play, talk, pray, nor work together. As a result, stability and discipline, so desperately needed for a well-ordered society, are not developed.

Science has contributed to moral chaos in direct and indirect ways. Most of the beneficial developments of science can be— and have been—used for harmful purposes. Automobiles have been turned into bedrooms on wheels to harbor unmarried couples in sexual intercourse. Jet planes whisk persons from an area where they are known to places where lack of identity eases moral restraint. Contraceptive pills and penicillin have made it "safe" to violate existing sex codes. Atomic weapons contribute to the despair of the day. Mass communication media bombard people with a bewildering variety of ethical concepts, leaving them morally confused. Many people today are exposed to more violence and sexual perversion in a week than a person living a hundred years ago was exposed to in a lifetime.

Science has also contributed to moral confusion by developing a whole array of items demanding moral decisions for which there has been little preparation. The atomic bomb threw the whole picture of war into a new perspective. Artificial insemination poses an ethical problem not faced by Biblical writers. The development of a contraceptive pill has created a furor of confusion over birth control among many, especially Roman Catholics. The whole social development of modern times with its accompanying problems is largely the result of science.

Science has had another and more subtle effect on morals. The stuff of science is the material world. The method of science is experiment. Science demands constant questioning. It is reluctant to state that anything is absolutely true. The scientific method has proved spectacularly successful. Men generally have accepted the scientific approach and have endeavored to apply it to other fields, such as religion and ethics.

The effects of the scientific revolution on ethical standards has been staggering. The foundation of the standards—religion—as well as the standards themselves has been shaken. Science did not set out to do this. The assault was not planned and carried out with forethought and malice. It has come simply because of what the scientific method is.

Since matter is the stuff of science, matter becomes the center of life in a scientifically oriented culture. By simply being itself, science stimulates materialism. Its achievements are in the material realm and men glory in them. As men turn more and more to the material, their thoughts are less and less of the spiritual. For most men of this new age, the supernatural is doubted or ignored. There seems to be less and less need for God.

The questioning spirit of science is quickly caught and applied to all of life, even to religion and ethics. The questioning spirit is accompanied by a rebellion against authority and a refusal to accept pronouncements without proof. The proof which is acceptable is also from the realm of science—experiment and fact. The tendency is to question once accepted moral principles and to experiment with alternatives. Since the spirit of science is openness, there is an unwillingness to propose or to accept any absolutes in regard to ethics.

Again and again, institutional Christianity has challenged the testing, experimenting, questioning, and theorizing of scientists. And again and again, in the eyes of the majority of the people, science has come out the victor. Convinced that religionists have been proved in error in some areas, deep questions have arisen concerning their position in regard to ethics.

For centuries the Christian faith, ethic, and Bible served as the basis of Western civilization. The rapid advance of science with a developing secular and material world view shook the religious foundations. Once largely the center of life, religion was relegated to one compartment in life—a compartment not necessarily related to conduct.

However, there was a general reluctance to let go of the ethic. So the cry became, "Give us the ethic of Jesus without the religion of Jesus." But the attempt to follow the teachings of Jesus apart from faith in Him was an experiment doomed to failure. It was like trying to build a skyscraper without a foundation or to grow a flower without roots. Disillusionment was bound to come—and has. Now even the Christian standards are often labeled as irrelevant, outdated, and, in some instances, immoral.

Regardless of how it came to pass, the God-centered, Bible-based ethic which once held sway is under attack or, worse, is largely ignored. Obviously, in spite of lip service, Americans are not particularly impressed by or prone to follow former standards. Many of the codes of conduct developed in an agrarian, rural, isolated, sparsely populated, unscientific, individualistic society seem strangely out of place in an industrial, urban, cosmopolitan, scientific-minded, densely populated, collective society. As a result, there is a desperate search for new standards or at least a new interpretation of old standards.

In fact, the heart of the moral problem of the nation is the loss of old standards and the chaos of a transition time in search of new ones. Numerous ethical theories clamor for favor: "Right is what brings pleasure," "Right is what works," "Right is relative," "Right is what I want it to be," or "Right is what makes people more human." In spite of all the talk about a "new morality," no one ethical position has gained general acceptance, or promises to. The strongest contender appears to be secular humanism. Our culture is like a ship at sea without a rudder or an engine. We have nothing to give us guidance and no power to move us even if we knew where to go.

THE CHRISTIAN'S RESPONSE TO MORAL CRISIS

Faced with moral crisis, the Christian must beware of several tempting alternatives. We must not withdraw into the rufuge of a Sacred Society of Secluded Saints and piously cluck his tongue over the moral mess of his nation. His charge is to penetrate the world—as salt to bring healing and as light to show the way to sanity. He must not go about mouthing pious platitudes. His task is to communicate in meaningful terms the good news about God in Christ. He must not look for quick, easy solutions to enduring, complex problems. His is the task of a realistic appraisal of current evil and of an equally realistic response. He must not suffer from the paralysis of analysis. His challenge is to act. He must not launch an indiscriminate attack on all the evil around him. His fights must be picked with care so as to accomplish the most good. He must not depend solely on his own power and ability. His strength is in the Lord. Yet he must not shrug off his responsibility with superpious statements such as, "The only answer to the moral crisis is the second coming of the Lord." His responsibility is to work to lift the world Godward. He must not give up when his efforts do not produce perfection. His calling is to be faithful to the task assigned him by God.

If he is to help his morally depressed society, the Christian must understand clearly the nature of the Christian faith and ethic. Cold moralism is an inadequate answer to moral crisis. Hope rests, not in new ethical standards, but in new men. Man's desperate moral illness can only be cured by his becoming a new creation in Christ. No mere conformity to a code of conduct will suffice. The need is the commitment of faith to a Person.

The uniqueness of the Christian ethic rests, not in moral propositions, but in the person of Christ. Jesus is so unique as to be the answer to man's moral dilemma. He is the only one who is God come to be man. Amid the babble of moral confusion, He is the living example of what a man ought to be. He is the only one who died to set men free from the paralyzing guilt of moral failure. He is the one who rose from the dead with the promise, "I am with you alway." As the living and indwelling Christ, He provides the dynamic for a man's doing what he knows he ought to do (Gal. 2:20).

The Christian who loves as Christ loves finds himself inescapably involved in all kinds of efforts to snatch his neighbor from moral and spiritual ruin. By what he says and by what he does, he shares his experience of life with Christ. He invites others to turn from their present pattern of life and to trust and follow Christ. Becoming an adequate witness is the Christian's most basic response to moral crisis. It should not be his only response, however.

The Christian should not only understand the nature of the Christian ethic and apply it to his own life, but he should also be able to communicate why the Christian approach to ethics is superior. In the arena of public discussion he should not abdicate. Besieged by reminders of moral failures by churches and churchmen, ridiculed for professing a better brand of morality than is practiced, informed that morality is a private affair, pestered by innuendoes, half-truths, and sarcasm the Christian is tempted to turn to the sanctuary of silence. But he must not. In the battle for men's minds he must make certain that the Christian message is clearly and persuasively presented.

Home, church, community, and government must all be included in the Christian's response to the moral crisis. He should strive to make his own home an island of stability in a sea of moral chaos. Special care should be taken to root children solidly in the Christian approach to moral decision-making.

Within the churches Christians should minister to the total needs of people, encourage preaching and teaching related to the moral issues of the day, constantly evaluate the program of the church in the light of a changing culture, and stimulate fellow Christians to assume responsible roles in community life.

Dedicated Christians, able in leadership, should seek service in places of community responsibility. In business, labor unions, civic clubs, communications, publishing, education, government, and professional organizations, Christians can contribute to the moral tone of the community. In addition, they should encourage the passing and enforcement of laws to curtail, if not control, all that is harmful to persons.

Understanding his own trust in Christ and its relation to life, applying the ethical demands of Jesus to his own life, praying for himself and for his neighbor, meaningfully communicating Christ to others, working in his home, church, community, and government to create a healthy moral climate—this is the needed Christian response to Moral Crisis, U.S.A.